THE DOCTRINE OF THE SEPARATION OF
POWERS AND ITS PRESENT-DAY SIGNIFICANCE

The Doctrine of the Separation of Powers and Its Present-Day Significance

by

Arthur T. Vanderbilt

UNIVERSITY OF NEBRASKA PRESS / LINCOLN

INTRODUCTION

This volume of lectures by Chief Justice Vanderbilt is the only modern comprehensive statement and analysis of the constitutional doctrine of the separation of governmental powers. As such, it should be required reading for all students of government or law. This study of the present significance of separated powers together with Professor Sharp's historical review[1] form a complete survey of the topic by two outstanding legal scholars. An introduction is added only to give a rigorous definition of the doctrine in its constitutional context.

Chief Justice Vanderbilt was not an impartial student of the doctrine of separation of powers; he was one of its leading protagonists. The constitutional separation of governmental powers was designed to effect a system of checks by each department on the other two. As a constitutional principle for the protection of individual liberty against arbitrary actions of governmental officials, it ranks equal to the guarantees in Sections 9 and 10 of Article I of the Constitution and in the first nine amendments. As noted by Chief Justice Vanderbilt (p. 35), the separation of powers cannot by itself guarantee constitutional democracy, but it is clearly one of the necessary elements.

The doctrine of the separation of powers is a general constitutional principle, and it was neither conceived nor has it ever operated as a rigid rule (p. 50). The special cases where one branch performs some particular function of another branch are both explicit and implied by the very nature of government. But the special cases are determinable and limited, for the rule of separation of powers is meaningless if it can be circumvented completely. The general nature of the separation of powers will be discussed first, followed by the four classes of special cases.

The fundamental idea of separation of powers is (with specified exceptions) the initial vesting of the powers of government in three separate and independent departments, the legislative, executive and judicial.[2] The first essential of independence is that persons holding office in one department do not owe their tenure to the will or preferences of persons in another of the branches.[3] Thus under the United States Constitution, the President and Members of Congress are continued in office or not at the will of the electorate at general elections.[4] And the federal judges hold office during good behavior, and their compensation may not be reduced.[5] The second essential of independence is that officials in one department may not concurrently hold office in either of the other two departments,[6] and may not usurp or encroach upon the powers which the Constitution clearly assigns to another department.[7]

Chief Justice Vanderbilt emphasizes (p. 9) that the independence of the judiciary is the best test of the actuality of the rights of the individual.[8] The separation of governmental powers under our Constitution is thus found in its most strict and complete form in separation of the judiciary from the legislative and executive. Under our system of judicial supremacy, the judiciary is the operative check on possible arbitrary action by legislatures or executive officers. The effectiveness of the judicial bar to arbitrary and oppressive government can be guaranteed only by a judiciary that is free from executive or legislative control.[9] In the classic statement of Lord Coke: "No man may be a judge in his own cause."[10] Neither the legislature which has exercised the sovereign law-making power in enacting a statute nor the executive officers charged with enforcing a statute may sit in judgment of a defendant charged with violating the statute. For both the legislature and executive, in their efforts to govern, have a vested and therefore biased interest in unlimited statutory enforcement.[11] They cannot be impartial judges of the constitutional limitations on their own acts.[12] Only an independent judiciary can perform this function.

First special case: checks in the Constitution to balance powers.

The constitutional purpose of preventing arbitrary abuse of power by officials was to be accomplished through separation of powers so that each independent branch of government would operate as a check on the other two. To effect the checking function, the Constitution allocates to each of the three departments some specific powers which are usually peculiar to one of the other departments. The President is given limited control over the legislative function through use of the veto.[13] The Vice President also has a legislative function as President of the Senate and is empowered to vote when they are equally divided.[14] The President is given limited control over the judiciary in criminal cases by his power to grant reprieves and pardons for federal offenses.[15]

The Congress has a comprehensive control over the executive in its general legislative power to amend or repeal statutes that had authorized particular executive action. The Senate controls the executive in its power of approval over treaties and over appointments by the President of ambassadors, judges, and other officers of the United States.[16] Each House may punish its own members for contempt and the Senate is allocated one other judicial function, the sole power to try impeachments.[17]

The judiciary, although not allocated specific executive power or general supervisory power over the executive, is able to see that the executive performs duties which have clearly been assigned to it by the Constitution through use of its general equitable jurisdiction to issue mandamus against executive officers.[18] Probably the most important judicial check on the misuse of executive power is the requirement of full hearing and fair procedure in our trial courts before any person is deprived of his legal rights, the due process limitation.[19] And though it is not stated in the Constitution, the judiciary controls legislative action through its power to declare laws unconstitutional.[20]

Second special case: incidental powers necessary to carry on allocated constitutional power.

It is often necessary for officials in one department, for the full and proper discharge of their duties, to perform acts which usually belong to one of the other two departments. Both the judiciary and the executive must exercise some minimal legislative power in making rules for the orderly conduct of their departments. It is said that courts have an inherent rule-making power, limited by the procedure statutes enacted by the legislature.[21] The rules and regulations of an executive department for the discharge of its duties are usually made pursuant to a general statute delegating such functions.[22] Both courts and legislatures must also engage in some executive or administrative activities in discharging their duties. Thus, there is a power to employ and discharge clerks, deputies and assistants necessary to carry on the judicial[23] and legislative[24] functions. It is significant that neither the legislature nor the executive need perform any judicial acts as an incident to discharging their functions.

Third special case: separation of powers in Federal Constitution does not apply to states.

It is clear that the separation of powers in the Federal Constitution applies only to Federal government. The Fourteenth Amendment does not require a separation of powers in state governments.[25] Nor does Article IV, Section 4 of the Constitution, which guarantees to every state a republican form of government, prevent combined powers in the states.[26] Thus the states are free to distribute the powers of their governments as they will and their state constitutions are the only constraint on state legislatures limiting concentration of powers in a single person or agency. This does not mean that the powers of government are combined in the states. All fifty of the state constitutions vest the legislative, executive, and judicial powers in separate departments.[27] Thirty-six states forbid any of the three departments from exercising powers properly belonging to another department. Most state constitutions, however, have exceptions to the stated rule of absolute separation, as was noted for the Federal Constitution in the previous two sections.

Fourth special case: delegation of secondary legislative functions.

The one power under which some functions must by

their very nature be delegable to other agencies of government is the legislative power.[28] The legislative power is the
sovereign power to make general rules of conduct for the
political community enforceable in the future by the physical
force of the state.[29] The legislature, though vested with this
power, is basically a duty-assigning body, since in making law
it directs the executive to do such acts as are necessary to
achieve the results required by the statute.[30] But the degree of
generality in statutes varies. Controversy between factions in
a legislature may cause them to choose more general language
as a compromise.[31] In our technically complex society, the
legislature may lack the skill to develop the detailed rules
that will carry out a general regulatory policy.[32] And dynamic
changes in industry may make it essential that some detailed
rules be under almost constant change.[33] To the extent that
the legislature leaves for the executive the making of detailed
secondary rules in enforcing a statute, there is necessarily a
delegation of some legislative functions. And it can be argued
that in the Constitution Congress is given explicit authority
to make such secondary delegations.[34]

Before turning to the constitutional aspects, it should be
noted that the analogies from agency law do not apply to the
constitutional vesting of the sovereign coercive power of government in the legislature, executive and judiciary.[35] The
people as electors are not principals, delegating authority to
government to do acts they could do themselves. Governing
one another is something which they could not do themselves,
without government. Congressmen are not agents. They are
not bound to follow directions from any single elector or
group of electors. And their power is sufficient to pass laws
that force a large minority of electors to do acts which those
electors do not wish to do. For these reasons, the ancient
agency maxim prohibiting the unauthorized subdelegation of
agency power has no application to the election of legislatures
and their delegation of rule-making functions to administrative agencies.[36]

The vesting of sovereign legislative power in a legislature

is more closely analogous to the creation of a trust in those persons elected to office. For in a democracy it is a public trust to govern by use of the state's monopoly on the physical force of organized society for the benefit of the society as a whole.[37] Following the trust analogy it is significant that a trustee may not delegate his general discretionary powers to an agent.[38] He may, however, as long as he retains the full responsibility, employ agents where reasonably necessary to carry out his duties and especially for matters in which he is not experienced.[39] There is a clear application of these rules in democratic government. In our Constitution, the people have vested the legislative power in the Congress and have thus given it the primary law-making task.[40] Surely this will forbid the delegation by Congress to the executive or judiciary of the authority to exercise its entire legislative power or its entire power over any particular subject matter, for such unlimited delegation would reallocate the constitutional distribution of governmental powers.[41] And the legislature has not been given the constitutional power by itself to amend the constitution.[42]

The separation of powers into three independent branches thus incorporates a constitutional mandate to Congress that it alone may exercise the plenary legislative power in the sense that only Congress may adopt the primary rules of conduct for the nation. But this does not preclude the voluntary delegation by the Congress to the executive of the secondary or subsidiary rule-making functions.[43] Here the agency analogy seems to have force. A principal, in delegating specific contracting authority to his agent to act in a representative capacity for him, does not lose any of his own power to contract. He may intervene in the negotiations carried on by his agent or give special directions to the agent for the making of particular contracts.[44] The principal may at his will also terminate the representative authority of his agent.[45]

Similarly, the legislature, having exercised its constitutional power and duty to make the primary rules of conduct for the state, may delegate some of its functions by creating a partial agency in an executive department or administrative commission to make the more detailed secondary rules.[46] The statute which states the primary rules, the standards for regulatory control, in effect also states the scope of the partial agency.[47] The legislature retains the power, by amending or repealing the statute which created the agency, to change the agency's authority to make the secondary rules or to revoke the agency.[48] The legislature's sovereign law-making power, which includes plenary powers of control over administrative structure and procedure, is thus unimpaired by the delegation of secondary legislative functions.

It is significant that, in spite of the past and present confusion of many judges and scholars, the above rule of non-delegable legislative power but delegable secondary legislative functions has always been our law.[49] Chief Justice Vanderbilt quotes Madison (p. 50) as authority for the view that the blending of legislative and executive powers through limited voluntary delegation by the legislature is clearly constitutional. His insight into the nature of delegation, as opposed to unconstitutional usurpation, is a significant contribution to our understanding of the Constitution.

In contrast to the legislative power, the judicial functions are not delegable. Unlike the legislature, the judiciary is not a duty-assigning branch of government. Judges are appointed or elected for their personal qualifications to perform the judicial function. Unlike legislators, judges are not laymen chosen from the population as a whole. The judiciary is a true example of a body with specialized skills and technical knowledge. For this reason, the act of judging is unquestionably a personal duty.[50] Hence, any attempt by a judge to delegate his clearly judicial functions to a legislative or administrative agency would violate both his oath of office and the constitutional separation of powers.

The legislative and executive departments are subject to an analogous constitutional constraint. Under the Constitution they have not been vested with any general judicial power. *Ipso facto,* they also are constitutionally unable to delegate clearly judicial functions to administrative agencies.[51] From these constitutional premises, it necessarily follows that the courts may not acquiesce in legislative attempts to delegate to administrative agencies clearly judicial functions. Since the legislature has no judicial power to delegate, it would merely be directing the administrative officers to usurp judicial power. And the Supreme Court has held without exception that the constitutional separation of powers forbids the judiciary from approving the usurpation of judicial power by legislative or executive officers. This elementary logic prevails in all jurisdictions where the constitutions vest the entire judicial power in the courts.[52]

Chief Justice Vanderbilt's views on the current vitality of the doctrine of separation of powers received strong support in the *Youngstown* case[53] in the opinions of Justices Black, Frankfurter, Douglas, and Jackson. Separation of powers is not now nor has it ever been an impediment to effective government. It permits the delegation of secondary legislative functions where the legislature finds such delegation expedient for workable regulation. Yet it provides for an independent judiciary to guarantee due process of law when one may be deprived of existing legal rights. As noted in Chief Justice Vanderbilt's final lecture, judicial deference or restraint is inappropriate when the executive or legislature attempts to usurp judicial power or to abridge the personal rights, privileges and immunities that the Constitution explicitly protects. Chief Justice Vanderbilt has an undeniable answer for the enthusiastic public administrators or ivory-towered professors who say, "Separation of powers is passé; regulation must be quick and efficient; let the prosecutor be judge." His response is that the separation of powers is a constitutional cornerstone of individual liberty; pull out one cornerstone and the edifice will begin to crumble.

MICHAEL CONANT

University of California
Berkeley, California

NOTES

1. Sharp, *The Classical American Doctrine of "The Separation of Powers"*, 2 U. of Chi. L. Rev. 385 (1935).

2. "James Wilson, one of the framers of the Constitution and a justice of this court, in one of his law lectures said that the independence of each department required that its proceedings 'should be free from the remotest influence, direct or indirect, of either of the other two powers.' Andrews, The Works of James Wilson (1896), Vol. 1, p. 367. And the importance of such independence was similarly recognized by Mr. Justice Story when he said that in reference to each other neither of the departments 'ought to possess, directly or indirectly, an overruling influence in the administration of their respective powers.' 1 Story on the Constitution, (4th ed.) § 530. To the same effect, the Federalist (Madison) No. 48." O'Donoghue v. United States, 289 U. S. 516, 530-1 (1933).

3. Humphrey's Ex's v. United States, 295 U. S. 602 (1935), holding that the President may not at his will and in violation of statute remove a member of Federal Trade Commission, since FTC members perform subsidiary legislative functions.

4. Constitution, Article I, Sections 2-5 and Amendment XVII; Article II, Section 1 and Amendment XII. Each house shall be the Judge of the Elections, Returns and Qualfications of its own Members. Article I, Section 5.

5. Constitution, Article III, Section 1.

6. Constitution, Article I, Section 6.

7. The legislature may not usurp the executive or judicial powers. Springer v. Philippine Islands, 277 U. S. 189 (1928); Kilbourn v. Thompson, 103 U. S. 168 (1881). The executive may not usurp the legislative or judicial powers. Youngstown Sheet and Tube Co. v. Sawyer, 343 U. S. 579 (1952); Application of Yamashita, 327 U. S. 1 (1946). The judiciary may not usurp legislative or executive powers. United States v. National City Lines, 334 U. S. 573, 588–89 (1948); National City Bank of New York v. Republic of China, 348 U. S. 356, 358 (1955).

8. Effective separation of powers in England is said to date from the passage of a statute making judges removable from office only by impeachment by Parliament for misconduct. 12 Will. 3, c. 2 (1701). See Parker, *Historic Basis of Administrative Law: Separation of Powers and Judicial Supremacy*, 12 Rutgers L. Rev. 449, 450 (1958).

9. O'Donoghue v. United States, 289 U. S. 516, 531–534 (1933); Evans v. Gore, 253 U. S. 245, 248–253 (1920). "The complete independence of the courts of justice is pecularly essential in a limited constitution." Hamilton in Federalist No. 78 (1788) (p. 100 of Bourne ed., 1947).

10. For citations and discussions see Corwin, *The "Higher Law" Background of American Constitutional Law*, 42 Harv. L. Rev. 365, 370 (1929).

See Mason, Language of Dissent 303 (1959); Berger, *Removal of Judicial Functions from Federal Trade Commission to a Trade Court: A Reply to Mr. Kintner,* 59 Mich. L. Rev. 199, 204–6 (1960).

11. "[B]ias from strong and sincere conviction as to public policy may operate as a more serious disqualification than pecuniary interest." Gt. Britain, Report of the Committee on Ministers' Powers (Cmd. 4060, 1932). "Unlike a judge, who is theoretically neutral about government programs, an administrator often has an affirmative program to carry out; he often has a mission, a purpose, a policy." Professor Davis in Report of the Special Subcommittee on Legislative Oversight of the House Committee on Interstate and Foreign Commerce, Independent Regulatory Commissions, H. R. 2711, 85th Cong., 2d Sess., 1959, p. 78. See Cooper, *The Executive Department of Government and the Rule of Law,* 59 Mich. L. Rev. 515, 517–18 (1961).

12. "From a body which had even a partial agency in passing bad laws, we could rarely expect a disposition to temper and moderate them in the application. The same spirit which had operated in making them would be too apt to influence their construction; still less could it be expected that men who had infringed the Constitution in the character of legislators would be disposed to repair the breach in that of Judges." Hamilton in Federalist No. 81 (1788) (p. 121 of the Bourne ed., 1947).

13. Constitution, Article I, Section 7. See Corwin, The President: Office and Powers 337–342 (3rd ed., 1948).

14. Constitution, Article I, Section 3.

15. Constitution, Article II, Section 2. See Bozel v. United States, 139 F.2d 153, 156 (6th Cir. 1943), *cert. denied,* 321 U. S. 800 (1944).

16. Constitution, Article II, Section 2.

17. Constitution, Article I, Sections 5 and 3.

18. Constitution, Article III, Section 2. See Kendall v. United States, 12 Pet. (37 U. S.) 522 (1838).

19. Constitution, Amendments V and XIV. See Kwong Hai Chew v. Colding, 344 U. S. 590 (1953); Forkosch, *American Democracy and Procedural Due Process,* 24 Brooklyn L. Rev. 173 (1958).

20. Marbury v. Madison, 1 Cranch (5 U. S.) 137 (1803). See 1 Cooley, Constitutional Limitations 332–384 (8th ed., 1927).

21. McDonald v. Pless, 238 U. S. 264, 266–7 (1915). See Levin and Amsterdam, *Legislative Control Over Judicial Rule-Making: A Problem in Constitutional Revision,* 107 U. of Pa. L. Rev. 1 (1958); Pound, *The Rule-Making Power of the Courts,* 12 A.B.A.J. 599 (1926).

22. Boske v. Comingore, 177 U. S. 459, 469 (1900); Coffey v. Noel, 11 F. 2d 399, 401 (W. D. Va., 1926).

23. United States v. Swift, 139 F. 225, 228 (1st Cir. 1905); In re Utilities Power and Light Corp. 90 F.2d 798, 800 (7th Cir. 1937).

24. McGrain v. Daugherty 273 U. S. 135, 155 (1927); Spartanburg County v. Miller, 135 S. C. 348, 132 S. E. 673, 676–7 (1924).

25. Teamsters Union v. Hanke, 339 U. S. 470, 479 (1950); Dreyer v. Illinois, 187 U. S. 71 (1902).

26. Highland Farms Dairy v. Agnew, 300 U. S. 608, 612 (1937).

27. Dishman, State Constitutions: The Shape of the Document 2–3 (1960).

28. Cheadle, *The Delegation of Legislative Functions,* 27 Yale L. J. 892, 897 (1918).

29. Legislation involves the creation or extinction of general classes of rights or immunities for all persons who engage in the actions treated by the particular laws. See Dash v. Van Kleeck, 7 Johns. (N. Y. Ch.) 477, 502 (1811), per Kent, C. J.; San Diego Land & Town Co. v. Jasper, 189 U. S. 439, 440 (1903), per Holmes, J.; Prentis v. Atlantic Coast Line, 211 U. S. 210, 226 (1908), per Holmes, J. See Weeks, *Legislative Power versus Delegated Legislative Power,* 25 Geo. L. J. 314, 317–22 (1937); Green, *Separation of Governmental Powers,* 29 Yale L. J. 369, 373 (1920); Akzin, *The Concept of Legislation,* 21 Iowa L. Rev. 713, 734 (1936); Allen, Law in the Making 409 (6th ed., 1958).

30. Kendall v. United States, 12 Pet. (37 U. S.) 524, 610 (1838).

31. See Levi, *An Introduction to Legal Reasoning,* 15 U. of Chi. L. Rev. 501, 522 (1948); Miller, *Statutory Language and the Purposive Use of Ambiguity,* 42 Va. L. Rev. 23 (1956).

32. "Congress legislated on the subject as far as was reasonably practicable, and from the necessities of the case was compelled to leave to executive officers the duty of bringing about the result pointed out by the statute. To deny the power of Congress to delegate such a duty would, in effect, amount but to declaring that the plenary power vested in Congress to regulate foreign commerce could not be efficaciously exerted." Buttfield v. Stranahan, 192 U. S. 470, 496 (1904). See Goodnow, Principles of the Administrative Law of the United States 324 (1905); Freund, Standards of American Legislation 301 (1917); Rosenberry, *Administrative Law and the Constitution,* 23 Am. Pol. Sci. Rev. 32, 35 (1929).

33. Hampton & Co. v. United States, 276 U. S. 394, 404–6 (1928), holding delegation of power to President to adjust tariffs to equalize costs of production is constitutional.

34. "The Congress shall have the power ... to make all laws which shall be necessary and proper for carrying into Execution the foregoing Powers, and all other Powers vested by this Constitution in the Government of the United States, or in any Department or Officer thereof." Constitution, Article I, Section 8.

35. Compare Locke, Second Treatise of Civil Government § 141 (1690).

36. See Duff and Whiteside, *Delegata Potestas Non Potest Delegari: A Maxim of American Constitutional Law,* 14 Cornell L. Q. 168 (1929).

37. Locke, who was a Chancery secretary, emphasized that the relationship of the legislature to the governed was not one of contract, but

in the nature of a legal trust, a primary fiduciary relationship. Locke *Op. cit.*, note 35, secs. 149, 156, 221, 222, 240. See Gough, Locke's Political Philosophy 136–171 (1950). See Trist v. Child, 88 U. S. 441, 450 (1875); Taylor and Marshall v. Beckham (No. 1), 178 U. S. 548, 577 (1900); Driscoll v. Burlington-Bristol Co., 8 N. J. 433, 86A.2d 201, 221 (1952); Prescott v. Ferris, 251 App. Div. 113, 295 N. Y. S. 818, 825 (1937); Conley v. State, 46 Neb. 187, 64 N. W. 708, 710 (1895); In re Corliss, 11 R. I. 638, 642 (1876); Mechem on Public Officers § 16 (1890).

38. Meck v. Behrens, 141 Wash. 676, 252 P. 91, 50 A. L. R. 207 (1927); Washington Loan & Trust Co. v. Colby, 108 F.2d 743, 747 (App. D. C., 1939). See 2 Scott on Trusts sec. 171.1.

39. In re Barnes' Estates, 339 Pa. 88, 14 A.2d 274, 276 (1940); In re Whipple's Estate, 19 N. Y. S. 2d 105, 110 (1940); Ewing v. Foley, 115 Tex. 222, 280 S. W. 499, 500 (1926); Ex Parte Belchier, 27 E. R. 144 (1754). See 2 Scott on Trusts sec. 171.2.

40. Constitution, Article I, Section 2.

41. Panama Refining Co. v. Ryan, 293 U. S. 388, 421 (1935); A. L. A. Schechter Poultry Corp. v. United States, 295 U. S. 495, 529 (1935). "Congress cannot delegate any part of its legislative power except under the limitations of a prescribed standard." United States v. Chicago, M. St. P. & P. R. Co., 282 U. S. 311, 324 (1931).

42. See generally, Kedroff v. St. Nicholas Cathedral of Russian O. Ch., 344 U. S. 94, 107 (1952); Feely v. Sidney S. Schupper Interstate Haulng System, 72 F. Supp. 663, 667 (D. Md. 1947)

43. "That the legislative power of Congress cannot be delegated is, of course, clear. But Congress may declare its will, and after fixing a primary standard, devolve upon administrative officers the 'power to fill up the details' by prescribing administrative rules and regulations." United States v. Shreveport Grain & Elevator Co., 287 U. S. 77, 85 (1932).

44. Manufacturers Cas. Ins. Co. v. Martin-Lebreton Ins. A., 242 F.2d 951 (5th Cir. 1957); Shrewsbury v. Dupont Nat. Bank, 10 F.2d 632, 635 (App. D. C., 1925); Guggisberg v. Otsego County Co-op Ass'n., 258 Mich 553, 242 N. W. 2d 749, 750 (1932).

45. Shawver v. Ewing, 1 F.2d 423, 425 (8th Cir. 1924), *cert. denied,* 267 U. S. 601 (1925); Wilson Sullivan Co. v. International Paper M. R. Corp., 307 N. Y. 20, 119 N. E. 2d 573, 574 (1954); Elevator Operators and Starters' Union v. Newman, 30 Cal. 2d 799, 186 P.2d 1, 4 (1947). See Mechem, Outlines of the Law of Agency § 262 (4th ed., 1952).

46 "Necessity therefore fixes a point beyond which it is unreasonable and impracticable to compel Congress to prescribe detailed rules; it then becomes constitutionally sufficient if Congress clearly delineates the general policy, the public agency which is to apply it, and the boundaries of this delegated authority." American Power & Light Co. v. Securities & Exchange Comm. 329 U. S. 90, 105 (1946). See Sears, Roebuck & Co. v. Federal Trade Commission, 258 F. 307, 312 (7th Cir. 1919).

47. "The only authority conferred, or which could be conferred, by statute is to make regulations to carry out the purposes of the act—not to amend it." Miller v. United States, 294 U. S. 435, 440 (1935). "The Secretary of the Treasury is bound by law; and although, in the exercise of his discretion, he may adopt necessary forms and modes of giving effect to the law: yet, neither he nor those who act under him, can dispense with, or alter, any of its provisions." Tracy v. Swartout, 10 Pet. (35 U. S.) 80, 95 (1836).

48. "[A]change of law pending an administrative hearing must be followed in relation to permits for future acts. Otherwise the administrative body would issue orders contrary to the existing legislation." Ziffrin, Inc. v. United States, 318 U. S. 73, 78 (1943). See Stark v. Wickard, 321 U. S. 288, 310 (1944); Jaffe, *An Essay on Delegation of Legislative Power 1*, 47 Col. L. Rev. 359, 366 (1947).

49. Comer, Legislative Functions of National Administrative Authorities 121 (1957).

50. "One of the conditions which attaches to formal judicial proceedings is the rule that the judges shall personally hear and determine the matters to be decided. A judge who absented himself habitually from court and installed a friend as permanent *locum tenans,* or who handed over part of a trial to a subordinate, would not be permitted to remain on the bench." Robson, Justice and Administrative Law 68 (3d. ed., 1951).

51. Crowell v. Benson, 285 U. S. 22, 56–57 (1932); South Chicago Coal & Dock Co. v. Bassett, 104 F.2d 522, 525 (7th Cir. 1939), *aff'd* 309 U. S. 251 (1940); United States v. Sugar, 243 F. 423, 431 (E. D. Mich., 1917), *aff'd* 252 F. 79 (6th Cir. 1918), *cert. denied* 248 U. S. 578 (1918).

52. See e.g., Jersey Maid Milk Products Co. v. Brock, 13 Cal. 2d 620, 91P. 2d 577, 594 (1939); State v. Finch, 79 Idaho, 275, 315 P. 2d 529, 531–2 (1957). For cases in other states, see 16 C. J. S. Constitutional Law § 173, notes 76–77.

53. Youngstown Sheet and Tube Co. v. Sawyer, 343 U. S. 579 (1952).

Contents

AUTHOR'S INTRODUCTION

It is impossible in three lectures to say all that should be said about a doctrine that has engaged the attention of practical men of affairs as well as political philosophers for centuries. In recent decades it has been fashionable in certain quarters to pronounce funeral orations over the remains of the doctrine, but despite these attempts at burial it retains a remarkable vitality that tends to increase the more it is threatened. Instinctively people seem to sense in its violation, even in hours of danger, a threat to much that they hold dear in their daily life and they recognize in its observance the possibility of attaining the reign of law which alone can insure the freedom so essential to both the individual and to our civilization.

Our late nineteenth-century fling at empire-building, two world wars, a worldwide cold war with the red part of the world necessitating unparalled expenditures at home and abroad and the Korean War, have profoundly affected our accustomed way of life, economically, socially, and intellectually. In addition to these international complications, big business ever growing bigger, powerful labor unions ever waxing more powerful, and the ever-increasing popular demand for governmental services undreamed of a half century ago have brought about a tremendous increase in governmental activities, especially at the national level. As a result our government has become so complex that it is quite literally a government that nobody knows. This is bad for government and it is bad for the people. There is a point, moreover, beyond which mere size inevitably spells inefficiency and there is a limit to what a single finite mind, whether president, cabinet officer or general, can successfully undertake. Nor are these all of the difficulties confronting government as óne of the great instrumentalities of civilizatioṇ. The long continued wasting of our natural resources in peace as well as in war, unbalanced budgets over many years, the vast increase in the public debt and the growth of communism: all these are additional factors threatening us with a permanent state of emergency that is not conducive to individual liberty or a sound civilization.

It is against this background of international and national conditions that I have attempted to appraise the present-day significance of the doctrine of the separation of powers. The gigantic problems confronting us are not impossible of solution. Individual freedom and the progress of civilization are attainable, but only if each of the three branches of government conforms to the constitutional principles of the separation of powers. This they will do only if the people so will. The problem in the first instance thus becomes one of popular education in the fundamental principles of free government. Among these principles there is none more significant today than the doctrine of the separation of powers.

ANALYSIS

THE DOCTRINE OF THE SEPARATION OF
POWERS AND ITS PRESENT-DAY SIGNIFICANCE

THE DOCTRINE OF THE SEPARATION OF POWERS VIEWED COMPARATIVELY AND HISTORICALLY

M R. Justice Holmes once termed Roscoe Pound a uniquity. He is equally a ubiquity, for it would be difficult to find a field in the law that the former Director of the Botanical Society of Nebraska has not explored and charted with the skill of a natural scientist. But his genius does not stop there. Mere learning as such has never interested him. His encyclopedic grasp of the law has not been employed merely in describing or explaining the law as it is or has been; on the contrary, his penetrating insight into the law has been consistently devoted to pointing out the course to be followed to serve the needs of the time. "The Schoolmaster of the American Bar," as he has long been affectionately known to the profession, has, I suspect, enjoyed the appellation, for it gives recognition to the motive that has guided his life in the law. As Sir Maurice Sheldon Amos, himself a distinguished master of comparative law, put it in summarizing Dean Pound's teachings:

The main burden of Pound's exhortation may be summed up as follows: What we think, and write, and teach about the law is a matter of practical importance, for the conceptions which gain ascendancy in the community as to the significance and the mission of the law mould and inspire the actions of the legislator and the judges. Upon the legal profession in each country there devolves then a responsibility, the due sense of which has for some long time past been in abeyance, the responsibility for thinking and advising the nation as a profession. This responsibility lies less immediately upon the courts, since they must "go with the main body, not with the advance guard"; but it lies upon all those who have a less immediate responsibility for the preservation of the specious appearance of immutability, to con the chart, to determine at frequent intervals our latitude and longitude, and to lay the course for the next port. We want far more information, more statistics; for lawyers, like doctors, know too little of the subsequent fate of the lives and concerns in which for a moment they have intervened; and if I may finish with a controversial matter, it is to say that though his writings are primarily addressed to his own countrymen, no English reader who takes Pound's message at all to heart will fail to discern between the lines, on almost every page, the words "wanted, a Department of Justice," in default of which there is some ground for the fear that a justly impatient community will one day send us all about our business.[1]

Outweighing even his scholarly writings, which stand unrivaled in breadth and depth, Dean Pound's greatest contribution to the law is that he has awakened many members of a once complacent profession to a sense of their individual responsibility for the future of the law in a rapidly changing society.[2] It is with a keen

[1] *Roscoe Pound* by Sir Maurice Sheldon Amos, Quain Professor of Comparative Law in the University of London, in *Modern Theories of Law* (London, 1933).

[2] This mission was first revealed to the American Bar Association at its

sense of my indebtedness to him and of his many acts of friendship over the years that I have ventured to accept the invitation to deliver these lectures named in honor of the foremost legal scholar of the twentieth century.

On his recommendation I have taken as my subject The Doctrine of the Separation of Powers, a topic which has fascinated me since my law school days. I can think of no subject in the law of greater practical importance in the distraught age in which we are living and struggling, with personal government on the rise the world over. In saying so, however, I am not unmindful that there are those who entertain other notions concerning the doctrine. Indeed, James M. Landis, Dean Pound's successor at the Harvard Law School, a former chairman of the Securities and Exchange Commission and a protagonist of administrative justice, brushes the doctrine aside as the work of an "Aristotelian theoretician" and "a page of theory in Montesquieu." [3] In his lectures on *The Administrative Process* he ridicules the doctrine:

> Separation of powers as a political maxim is old; but as a principle of government, sanctified by being elevated to the constitutional level and embroidered by pontifical moral phrases, it has a distinctly American flavor. Our British cousins discover it now and then as they find that its preachment fits some practical or political need. But it was left to us to hallow the tripartite ideal of government, wherein all power delegated by the people was in the purported interests of liberty divided neatly between legislative, executive, and judicial.[4]

annual meeting in St. Paul in 1906 in an address entitled *The Causes of Dissatisfaction with the Administration of Justice,* 29 A. B. A. Rep. 397, reprinted in 20 J. Am. Jud. Soc'y 178 (1937) with a stirring introduction by Dean John H. Wigmore entitled *The Spark That Kindled the White Flame of Progress.*

[3] *Administrative Agencies in Government,* Dun's Report 7 (Nov. 1932).

[4] Introduction 1-2 (New Haven, 1938).

These views are in marked contrast to those of the Founding Fathers. Washington, in his Farewell Address, warned: "The spirit of encroachment tends to consolidate the powers of all the departments in one, and thus to create, whatever the form of government, a real despotism." [5] John Adams reasoned: "It is by balancing each of these three powers against the other two, that the efforts in human nature toward tyranny can alone be checked and restrained, and any degree of freedom preserved in the Constitution." [6] Jefferson was of the same mind: "The concentrating of these in the same hand is precisely the definition of despotic government. It will be no alleviation that these powers will be exercised by a plurality of hands and not by a single one; 173 despots would surely be as oppressive as one." [7] Madison was equally emphatic: "The accumulation of all powers, legislative, executive, and judiciary, in the same hands, whether of one, a few, or many, and whether hereditary, self-appointed, or elective, may justly be pronounced the very definition of tyranny." [8] No concept of government was so unanimously accepted by all the statesmen whose genius brought into being the American nation as was the doctrine of the separation of governmental powers. Nor was a belief in the doctrine peculiar to America. According to Holdsworth, the great English legal historian:

[5] As reprinted in XIII *Writings of George Washington* 277, 306 (Ford ed., New York, 1892).

[6] In a letter to Richard Henry Lee dated 15 Nov. 1775, and reprinted in IV *Works of John Adams* 185, 186 (Chas. F. Adams ed., Boston, 1851).

[7] *Notes on Virginia,* originally published in 1784 and reprinted in III *Writings of Thomas Jefferson* 85, 223-224 (Ford ed., New York, 1894).

[8] *The Federalist No. 47,* originally published in the New York Packet Feb. 1, 1778, as reprinted by the Nat. Home Lib. Foundation with an introduction by Earle in *The Federalist* 312, 313 (Sesquicentennial ed., Washington, D. C. 1938).

If a lawyer, a statesman, or a political philosopher of the eighteenth century had been asked what was, in his opinion, the most distinctive feature of the British constitution, he would have replied that its most distinctive feature was the separation of the powers of the different organs of government.[9]

And as authorities he cites Halifax, Atterbury, Horace Walpole, Voltaire, de Lolme, Vattell, Hardwicke, Paley and Blackstone, an impressive galaxy indeed.[10]

Nor does Dean Landis confine his attack to the doctrine itself. Anybody who supports the doctrine or is critical of the "administrative process" as Landis conceives it may expect a similar pommelling at his hands. In 1935 President Roosevelt appointed a distinguished Committee on Administrative Management, which reported in 1937. In transmitting the report to the Congress the President said: "I have examined the report carefully and thoughtfully and am convinced that it is a great document of permanent importance." But Dean Landis would have none of it, saying:

> Somewhat hysterically the President's Committee on Administrative Management has referred to the administrative process, as illustrated by the existing independent regulatory commissions, as a "fourth branch" of the government. Its sweeping condemnation of the process seems to proceed almost upon the mystical hypothesis that the number "four" bespeaks evil or waste as contrasted with some beneficence emanating from the number "three." The desirability of four, five, or six "branches" of government would seem to be a problem determinable, not in the light of numerology but rather against a background of what we now expect government to do.[11]

[9] X *History of English Law* 713 (Boston, 1938).
[10] *Id.,* 714–716.
[11] *The Administrative Process, op. cit.* 49.

In like fashion and in phrases that tempt one to underscoring he attacks the judiciary and the legislature:

> The administrative process has often to survive in an atmosphere charged with resentment of its significance and of its force. Its *bending* of judicial doctrine and procedure to *realistic curvatures* tends sometimes to offend the courts that supervise its activities. Its relative isolation from the popular democratic processes occasionally arouses the antagonism of legislators who themselves may wish to play a controlling part in some activity subject to its purview.[12]

Landis' ideal of governmental administrative organization is the organization of an industrial corporation:

> As the governance of industry, bent upon the shaping of adequate policies and the development of means for their execution, vests powers to this end without regard to the creation of agencies theoretically independent of each other, so when government concerns itself with the stability of an industry it is only intelligent realism for it to follow the industrial rather than the political analogue.[13]

He perceives no necessity for any distinction between the management of an industrial enterprise and the management of an administrative agency authorized to regulate some aspect of industry.

I have cited these criticisms of the doctrine of the separation of powers by an outstanding spokesman for the administrative process not because they are unique—Landis is but one of a large school and his point of view could be duplicated a score of times —but to indicate the heat which any discussion of the doctrine is likely to occasion. The heat generated by jurisdictional conflicts,

---

[12] *Ibid.*
[13] *Id.*, 11–12.

whether they be of courts or of labor unions or of racketeers, is likely to be quite as intense as that aroused by political or religious controversies, and we must be on guard if we are simply seeking for light on this vital problem. One runs great risks if he espouses a moderate view on the subject. Judge Jerome Frank can scarcely be termed a defender of the existing order in the courts. His book *If Men Were Angels*[14] was designed, first, to defend the administrative agencies from attacks on them by opponents of administrative absolutism and, second, to come to the aid of the realists in their attacks on the courts. Alas for him, a capable reviewer finds that he has not kept the faith and regretfully takes him to task:

> One leaves the book with an all-persuasive impression that Frank has undergone a deep-sea change through his experiences as Chairman of the SEC and as judge. He now places a great value on "adequately worded statutes limiting discretion, proper rules of procedure, sufficient subjection to judicial correction." He takes pains to avoid the charge of nihilism or antinomianism. He is more prone to cite Aristotle than Freud. A time there was when Jerome Frank was the Robinson Jeffers of jurisprudence. It is hardly in order, however, to expect a judge of the United States circuit court of appeals to live on locusts and wild honey, to carry fire in his bosom and walk upon hot coals. "Wisdom hath builded her house; she hath hewn out her seven pillars; she hath killed her beasts; she hath mingled her wine." [15]

The protagonists of the administrative process in this country are not the only ones who are violently opposed to the doctrine of the separation of powers. Andrei Y. Vyshinsky, formerly attorney general and presently minister of foreign affairs of Russia

[14] New York, 1942.
[15] Konvitz, 56 Harv. L. Rev. 1020, 1022 (1943).

and regarded in Russia as a leading authority on Soviet law, writes:

> From top to bottom the Soviet social order is penetrated by the single general spirit of the oneness of the authority of the toiler. The program of the All-Union Communist Party (of Bolsheviks) rejects the bourgeois principle of separation of powers.[16]

> We do not have the separation of powers but the distribution of functions. . . . This is nothing in common with the Montesquieu doctrine.[17]

> In fact, the history of the capitalist world does not know any actual separation of powers; separation of powers has never existed.[18]

> Delimitation of their functions, given out as the separation of powers, is nothing more than the hegemony of the executive power over the legislative, a limitation of the rights of parliaments.[19]

Under the Soviet system, according to Vyshinsky, the Presidium, a body accountable directly to the legislature, interprets the laws of the legislature.[20] It is interesting to note that under the 1924 Constitution the Soviet Supreme Court did have certain powers over the interpretation of statutes, but in the 1936 Constitution this right was given solely to the Presidium.[21] Although

---

[16] *The Law of the Soviet State* 318 (New York, 1948), translated by Babb.

[17] *The Stalin Constitution,* Socialist Legality Nos. 8/9, 12 (in Russian, 1936), quoted in I. Gsovski, *Soviet Constitutional Law* 74 (Ann Arbor, 1948).

[18] I Vyshinsky and Undrevich, *Soviet Constitutional Law* 296 (in Russian, 1938), quoted in Gsovski, *op. cit.,* 75 n.

[19] *The Law of the Soviet State, op. cit.,* 314.

[20] *Id.,* 339.

[21] *Id.,* 340. See also Hazard, *The Soviet Constitution: An Introduction,* 3 Lawyers Guild Rev. 27, 36, 41 (Nov., Dec., 1943).

the Presidium now has authority to interpret the law, in practice it has rarely done so, preferring instead to issue decrees changing the law or even the Constitution itself,[22] a device extensively used not only by Stalin in Russia but, as we shall see, by Hitler in making the transition from the Weimar Republic to the Third Reich.

The independence of the judiciary in any system of law is the best test of the actuality of the rights of the individual. Although the Soviet Constitution declares that "Judges are independent and subject only to the law," [23] Vladimir Gsovski, Chief of the Foreign Law Section of the Library of Congress, points out that soviet writers, prior to the 1936 Constitution, expressed views incompatible with the doctrine of the independence of the courts.[24] But since the 1936 Constitution, they claim that soviet judges "are independent in the true and direct meaning of the word."[25] Soviet writers also point out that their judges are elected by the people in direct elections,[26] but Harold J. Berman of the Harvard Law School faculty notes, significantly, that although the constitutional provisions for judicial elections date back to 1936, the first elections were actually held in 1949.[27] Moreover, the courts are bound to play their part in preserving the political ideology of the Soviet Union. Thus Vyshinsky in discussing the role of the courts says: "The court in the USSR is an organ preserving the interests

[22] Gsovski, *op. cit.,* 72, 265.

[23] *Constitution of the Union of Soviet Socialist Republics* (1936) as amended through June 1, 1949, Art. 112 (English ed. published by Am. Russ. Inst., New York, 1950).

[24] Gsovski, *op. cit.,* 247–250.

[25] *Soviet Constitutional Law* 462 (in Russian, 1938), quoted in Gsovski, *op. cit.,* 252. Vyshinsky, *The Law of the Soviet State, op. cit.,* 499, 513.

[26] Vyshinsky, *The Law of the Soviet State, op. cit.,* 512, U.S.S.R. Const. *op. cit.,* Art. 109. Note also Art. 105: the Supreme Court is elected by the Supreme Soviet.

[27] *Justice in Russia* 167 (Cambridge, 1950).

of the socialist state and Soviet citizens. . . . This the court accomplishes by destroying without pity all the foes of the people in whatsoever form they manifest their criminal encroachments upon socialism." [28] Vyshinsky further reveals soviet thinking as to the role of the courts in politics by saying: "Neither court nor criminal procedure is or could be outside politics. This means that the contents and form of judicial activities cannot avoid being subordinated to political class aims and strivings." [29] Commenting on this statement, Gsovski notes: "There is no use denying that unfortunately, in too many instances, in too many countries, the courts are open to political influences. But what singles out the soviet point of view is that such submission to political purposes is expected from the soviet 'independent' judge." [30]

The soviet judge is under the control of the Ministry of Justice which checks the decisions of the courts, decides whether to appeal, imposes disciplinary penalties on judges and recommends the dismissal of judges and the granting of rewards.[31] Gsovski in summing up the position of the soviet courts has this to say:

> The specific modest and subordinate position of the soviet court within the soviet machinery . . . is the real reason why the theoretic discussion by the soviet law fails to clarify the situation. . . . To accept such doctrines totally would mean to grant the soviet courts more authority than is compatible with the general concept of "the dictatorship of the proletariat" as the source of law. The dictatorship of the proletariat is no more logically reconcilable with a free and independent court as a law-creative force than any other dictatorship. The de-

[28] Vyshinsky, *The Law of the Soviet State, op. cit.,* 497–498.
[29] *The Theory of Evidence in the Soviet Law* 31 (in Russian, 1941) as quoted in Gsovski, *op. cit.,* 255.
[30] *Ibid.*
[31] *Op. cit.,* 252–253.

cision in a case is in the last analysis controlled by the policy of those official and semi-official agencies which exercise the dictatorship and not by precedents. Soviet cases offer rather examples of how problems have been decided in the past than reason for predicting a future decision. Any change in the policy of the government may interrupt the chain of precedent.[32]

The Soviet Constitution stresses the importance of the Supreme Soviet as being the highest organ of state power with exclusive legislative powers.[33] But as we have seen, the Presidium exercises legislative power and the Council of Ministers does likewise.[34] In actual practice, the law in effect in the Soviet Union is the most recent act—be it called a law, edict, decree, order, instruction, resolution or statute—of the Supreme Soviet, the Presidium, or the Council of Ministers.[35]

In order to fully comprehend the workings of the soviet government we must understand the role in the government of the Communist Party, the sole legal party in Russia.[36] The party is the all-pervasive force in the government which enforces its policy no matter which organ of government is doing the legislating, executing or adjudicating. Gsovski thus describes its function:

> The role of the Communist Party in the soviet State . . . is totally different from the role of a political party in a democratic country. The Communist Party appears as an essential, permanent element of the actual soviet government machinery. The party network is the framework of this machinery, holding tight its loose links. This explains why the unsettled and

[32] *Id.,* 79. See also Berman, *op. cit.,* 194.
[33] U.S.S.R. Const., *op. cit.,* Arts. 30, 32.
[34] *Id.,* Art. 66; Gsovski, *op. cit.,* 73.
[35] Gsovski, *op. cit.,* 75.
[36] Vyshinsky, *The Law of the Soviet State, op. cit.,* 627.

overlapping jurisdictions of the supreme government bodies do not obstruct the functioning of the whole system. The decisions are made on the party "top levels," which are fused with corresponding levels of the soviet hierarchy, and are then promulgated in the form of an act of one or another official government body such as the Council of Ministers, Supreme Soviet, or its Presidium. None of these is, in itself, an authority, but merely an enforcement agency for decisions made on the very top level of the Communist Party. The functioning of the supreme party authorities, the Central Committee of the Party, its Politbureau, and the Secretary General, is not governed by any law. The Communist Party is the important and vital element of the soviet government machinery but lies outside the legal frame of the soviet system. It is a permanent extra-legal element in the making of soviet laws and their enforcement.[37]

To quote Berman again:

Soviet propaganda has stressed the changes wrought in constitutional law since 1936. From the viewpoint of civil liberties and political democracy these changes are insignificant. They are overshadowed by the absolute supremacy of the Communist Party and particularly its Politburo, for whom terror continues to be an important instrument of policy. The 1936 Constitution is important only as a symbol of the stability and legality which the regime ardently seeks but for which it is unwilling to sacrifice its faith in force. One might say that the Constitution regularizes the external system of government, without much affecting the actual process of political decision.[38]

In these views of the place of the Communist Party in the Soviet state Gsovski concurs:

Visualizing the foundation of the soviet government as the dictatorship of the proletariat exercised in its name by the

[37] *Op. cit.*, 79. See also Nove, *op. cit.*, 22–24.
[38] *Op. cit.*, 43.

Communist Party, the authors of the soviet theory of government drew two conclusions. The Communist Party must have a monopoly on political activities, and the power of the government may not be restricted. Therefore, the methods of Western democracy designed to restrict the power of the government, such as the separation of powers, the doctrine of checks and balances, the principle of government by law, are denied by them.[39]

The plain truth is that no authoritarian regime can tolerate the limitations on its powers that are implicit in the doctrine of the separation of powers.

Equally significant is the story of how defects in the constitution of the Weimar Republic paved the way for the despotism of Hitler. According to Blachly and Oatman, who are outstanding American critics of the doctrine of the separation of powers:

The principle of separation of powers is nominally preserved in the German Constitution through the independent and separate election of the President, and the bestowal of his chief functions by the Constitution itself rather than by the legislature. (Parenthetically we may observe that the judiciary is not deemed worthy of mention by them.) For working purposes, however, this separation, which has had so many undesirable consequences in the United States, is overcome by the requirement of ministerial countersignature to acts of the President. Thus the parliamentary principle is enforced, that the executive branch of the government must be responsible to the legislature for every act, while at the same time the President preserves a certain personal and official independence of status.[40]

[39] *Op. cit.,* 61–62.
[40] *The Government and Administration of Germany* 99 (Baltimore, 1928).

This view of the Constitution of the Weimar Republic, however, neglects the key position of Article 48 which provided that:

> If the public safety and order in the German Reich are seriously disturbed or endangered, the national President may take the measures necessary for the restoration of public safety and order, and may intervene if necessary with the assistance of the armed forces. For this purpose he may temporarily set aside in whole or in part, the fundamental rights established in Articles 114, 115, 117, 118, 123, 124 and 153.

> The national President must immediately inform the Reichstag of all measures taken in conformity with paragraph 1 or paragraph 2 of this Article. The measures are to be revoked upon the demand of the Reichstag.

The fundamental rights established in Articles 114, 115, 117, 118, 123, 124 and 153 that may be set aside by presidental edict under Article 48 are summarized by Blachly and Oatman as "personal freedom, inviolability of dwelling, secrecy of postal, telegraphic and telephonic communication, freedom of expression of opinion, freedom of assembly, freedom of association, and guarantees of property." [41] It is difficult to conceive of individual rights more vital than these, yet the Reichstag's check on the president's power to abrogate them was ineffective, for it came after the event.

The acts and edicts of the president, moreover, unfortunately were not restricted to executive measures. Although in the beginning there was some challenge to legislation by the president,[42] subsequent judicial decisions were unanimous in holding that the president had legislative powers under Article 48.[43] Even more

---

[41] *Op. cit.,* 75.

[42] Watkins, *The Failure of Constitutional Emergency Powers Under the German Republic* 99 (Cambridge, Mass., 1939).

[43] *Id.,* 19.

significant is the fact that the presidential finding of the existence of an emergency was never challenged by the courts; they were no help as a check on the powers of the president.[44] Under Article 25 of the Constitution, moreover, the president could always dissolve the Reichstag. Although Article 25 required that elections for the new Reichstag must be held no later than the sixtieth day after dissolution, as much as three months might elapse before the new Reichstag was actually elected and convened and during this period the president's power under Article 48 would go altogether unchallenged.[45]

It was these powers of the president which led to the destruction of the then existing government in Germany. In the spring of 1932 the aged Hindenburg was aproaching the end of his first seven-year term as president and Chancellor Bruning was using the president's powers under Article 48 in an attempt to preserve the existing government against the extremist elements represented by the National Socialist Party and the Communist Party. Bruning persuaded Hindenburg to run against Adolph Hitler and Hindenburg won. But shortly after his election Hindenburg, who had not interfered with Bruning in the past, demanded that Bruning stop certain of his policies of "agrarian Bolshevism" that Hindenburg felt were having an adverse effect on the Prussian landed aristocracy. Bruning resigned and a brief period of presidential government followed.[46] Franz von Papen, the next chancellor, continued to govern through the use of Article 48. He and Hindenburg thought alike and were no check on each other. Eventually he was replaced by General von Schleicher, who like Bruning was suddenly dismissed by the superannuated Hinden-

[44] *Id.*, 21.
[45] *Id.*, 22-23.
[46] *Id.*, 96–98.

burg. Hindenburg then appointed Adolph Hitler chancellor. This act marked the end of responsible government in Germany.[47]

To understand these events it is necessary to digress for a moment and consider the relationship between the German president and his chancellor and cabinet. Article 50 of the Constitution required that all ordinances and orders of the president be countersigned by the chancellor or a cabinet member concerned therewith. Article 53, however, gave the president the power to appoint and dismiss the chancellor and other cabinet members, while Article 54 provided that the chancellor and the cabinet must have the confidence of the Reichstag, being compelled to resign if that confidence were withdrawn by an express vote. Thus, while very broad powers were conferred on the president under Article 48, hereinbefore quoted, the exercise of these powers was not without controls. Writers have disagreed both as to the intended objective of these constitutional provisions and as to the practical effectiveness of the controls imposed by them,[48] but whatever the correct interpretation of the Weimar Constitution, presidential government without constitutional objection was plainly a fact during the period of the early 1930's.

Article 48 left little to be desired by anyone bent on destroying constitutional government while seeming to comply with the forms of law. Hitler first used Article 48 to gain a majority in the Reichstag by curtailing the right of the opposition to assemble, by restricting the press, by outlawing the Communist Party a few days before the election and by directing the police to ignore his

[47] Id., 99-107.

[48] Blachly and Oatman, op, cit., 92, 103-110; Friedrich, The Development of the Executive Power in Germany, 27 Am. Pol. Sci. Rev. 185, 198 (1933); Mattern, Principles of the Constitutional Jurisprudence of the German National Republic 388–389 (Baltimore, 1928); Rogers, Foerster, Schwarz, German Political Institutions, 47 Pol. Sci. Q. 321, 332 (1932).

terroristic campaign activities.[49] These methods netted Hitler's National Socialists 44% of the Reichstag, a workable parliamentary majority considering the number of parties, but unsatisfactory to a zealot whose party had always decried parliamentary government and promised absolutism to the electorate.[50] To obtain the desired two-thirds vote to pass an enabling act he invoked Article 48 to arrest all of the communist members of the Reichstag.[51] "At this crucial time there was no authority in Germany legally capable of challenging the discretion of the government. Article 48 had rendered its ultimate disservice to the Weimar Republic." [52]

Despite this ruthlessness Hitler's party acquired barely enough support to force through on March 23, 1933 an enabling act sardonically entitled the "Law for the Relief of the People and of the Reich" under which the National Socialist cabinet was given legislative authority for four years without the necessity of reporting to the Reichstag or of revoking acts at its demand as prescribed by Article 48. Even more, the act granted power to the cabinet to deviate from the Constitution itself, so long as the position of the Reichstag was not affected, meaningless language in view of the realities of the situation.[53] This act "marks the effective establishment of the Third Reich." [54]

With these dictatorial powers Hitler proceeded rapidly to eliminate the labor unions, both Social-Democratic and Catholic,

[49] Watkins, *op. cit.*, 109–118.

[50] *Id.*, 120–121.

[51] *Id.*, 121. While the Communist Party had been outlawed a few days before the last election, no attempt had been made to exclude its candidates from the ballot and the communists elected the third largest group of 81 members.

[52] *Id.*, 122.

[53] *Id.*, 120-126.

[54] *Id.*, 126.

the veterans organizations, the Social-Democratic Party, the German Nationalists (a party that had supported him), the Center Party, the Bavarian People's Party, and all Catholic parties. The National Socialists were thus the only legitimate party left in Germany.[55] Not content, Hitler on January 30, 1934, obtained the passage of a second enabling act, the "Law for the Reconstruction of the Reich," abolishing what little was left of German federalism and giving the cabinet the unlimited right "to determine new constitutional law." [56] From a legalistic point of view the establishment of absolutism should doubtless be reckoned from January 30, 1934.

The temporary German Constitution of 1949 has sought to overcome the defects of the Weimar Constitution with respect to the separation of powers. It provides:

(1) The Federal Republic of Germany is a democratic and social federal state. (2) All state authority emanates from the people. It shall be exercised by the people in elections and plebiscites and by means of separate legislative, executive and judicial organs. (3) Legislation shall be limited by the constitution, the executive and the administration of justice by legislation and the law.[57]

While there are provisions for emergency legislation in Article 81 of the 1949 Constitution, they are so complicated that we may not pause to quote them here. Suffice it to say that they do not seem to admit of the excesses possible under Article 48 of the Weimar Constitution.

---

[55] *Id.,* 128.
[56] *Ibid.*
[57] *Germany 1947–1949, The Story in Documents* 285, Dept. of State, Publication 3556, European and British Commonwealth Series 9 (released March, 1950). The text of the German Constitution is found at 283–305.

In French thinking the doctrine of the separation of governmental power is quite as fundamental as it is in ours, but it has been applied in a manner wholly foreign to us largely as a result of unfortunate experiences antedating the French Revolution. Says Professor Bernard Schwartz, an outstanding authority on comparative administrative law:

> Anglo-American constitutional history is a record of attempts by the legislature and courts to restrain excesses by the executive branch. French constitutional theory has, on the other hand, been influenced by the memory of constant obstruction of the executive branch by the *Parlements*—the common law courts of appeal under the *Ancien Regime*. Whether rightly or wrongly, it was felt that they had unduly opposed efforts at necessary administrative reforms in order to conserve their own privileges and prerogatives. It is . . . the memory of these struggles [that is, between the Parlements and the executive] and of the detrimental effect on the country's administration which explains the deep distrust with which subsequent French Constitution-makers viewed all judicial activities, and which resulted at the time of the First Revolution in a complete separation not only of the judicial and administrative functions, but also of the judicial and administrative jurisdictions.[58]

The Constituent Assembly of 1789 set out to destroy the Parlements.[59] Nor did it stop there; to prevent a recurrence of the evil they had caused it precluded the new courts it established from interfering with the work of the government by enacting the basic law of August 16-24, 1790:

---

[58] *A Common Lawyer Looks at Droit Administratif,* 29 Can. B. Rev. 121, 126 (1951). I am particularly indebted to my former student and colleague for the privilege of reading and making use of part of his forthcoming study of *French Administrative Law.*

[59] Waline, *Traité Elémentaire de Droit Administratif* 42 (Paris, 5th ed., 1950).

Judicial functions are and will always remain distinct from administrative functions. Judges may not, under penalty of forfeiture of office, interfere in any manner with the workings of administrative bodies, nor summon administrators before them in connection with the exercise of their functions.[60]

Accordingly a French citizen aggrieved by some action of his government could not go to court about it. He might file a humble petition either with the perpetrator of the act complained of or with his administrative superior, but in either event the administration was its own judge. The inadequacy of such a procedure is obvious, but where could one find a judge who was not precluded by the fundamental law from sitting in such matters? How did the French meet this difficulty? The Council of State started as an administrative body, but like the English chancellor, it evolved into a court—the supreme court of the French administrative system. While other branches of the Council of State exercise administrative and legislative functions, the judicial section has been a separate and important judicial entity since 1806 by decree of Napoleon and, as might be expected in such circumstances, it has developed the techniques and traditions of a true court. Thus France has come to have two distinct sets of courts, one dealing with private controversies, the other concerned with disputes with the government—and never the twain shall meet.[61]

There is another feature of the French interpretation of the separation of powers that is equally significant for us today. The French administration, unlike our executive departments and our administrative agencies, is endowed with inherent authority to promulgate regulations. In this country, as in England, adminis-

[60] Schwartz, *op. cit.*, 127.
[61] *Id.*, 125-138.

trative rule-making power has its great source in delegation to the executive branch by the legislative. Here the legislature may give, but it may also take away. But in France the situation is exactly as if the power of the American president to "take care that the laws are faithfully executed" were deemed to give a vast reservoir of power to do what is "necessary and proper"—to quote Article I of our Constitution relating to the legislative branch—for carrying into effect the laws of the United States. The French prime minister is the head of the executive branch of government and he is charged with the execution of the laws. Unlike our chief executive in the nation and in the state he has a broad, inherent, general rule-making power covering any matter deemed necessary to protect the public interest. His ministers, in turn, may also issue rules without statutory authority within their own sphere, and prefects and mayors have the same power locally. This rule-making power, however, by whomsoever exercised, is clearly subordinate to parliamentary legislation, just as legislation is subordinate to the Constitution.

There is another distinction between our separation of powers and that of the French that is even more fundamental. Theoretically there can be no delegation of legislative powers by the French Parliament.[62] Yet in practice the legislature by passing so-called "decree laws" has gone to the extent of giving the administration the power to alter statutes. A sample is the law of February 28, 1934:

The Government is authorized, until June 30, 1934, notwithstanding any laws to the contrary, to take, by decrees . . . , the economic measures which the balancing of the budget demands.

[62] Vedel, *Manuel Elémentaire de Droit Constitutionnel* 498 (Paris, 1949).

This delegation gives to the executive powers such as imposing new taxes or increasing old ones, powers which are expressly reserved to Parliament alone under French constitutional theory. In reality the restrictions placed on the action of the legislature by the French Constitution are not law, since they are not rules which in the last resort will be enforced by the courts. Their true character is that of maxims of political morality, which derive whatever strength they possess from being formally inscribed in the Constitution and from whatever support of public opinion may result therefrom.[63] American critics of judicial review of legislation may well ponder on the position of the French Parliament. The contrast between France and this country is thus summarized by Professor Schwartz:

> The French experience shows that a Constitution which cannot be judicially enforced contains but empty words. It is judicial review which ensures that the American Constitution is not violated and gives that instrument its practical meaning. It is the failure of the French courts to assert a review power over the constitutionality of acts of the legislature that has made the various Constitutions in France mere paper instruments.[64]

Nor have the French people, despite earnest endeavors, been able to find a way out of their constitutional difficulties. In 1946 the French amended their Constitution by expressly prohibiting the delegation of legislative power by Parliament, but the French courts continued to fail to assert a power to review legislation because the Constitution did not expressly provide for judicial review. They lacked a Chief Justice Marshall to make their constitution effective. The result was that the constitutional language

[63] Dicey, *Law of the Constitution* 135 (London, 9th ed., 1939).
[64] Schwartz, *French Administrative Law: A Comparative Study* (as yet unpublished).

against delegation of legislative power was rendered meaningless. In fact the first Parliament to sit under the 1946 Constitution passed the law of August 17, 1948, quite similar to the Act of February 28, 1934, authorizing the executive to take by decree any measures deemed necessary to deal with the economic situation. The law, moreover, expressly provides that any decrees so made may modify or replace existing legislation. Says Morange:

> Constitutional or not, the law of August 17, [1948] seems destined to be applied in a country where there is no judicial control of the constitutionality of laws and where such political control as has been provided for appears to be entirely illusory.[65]

For the reason that this study is limited to the recognition of the doctrine of separation of powers in written constitutions, we forego inquiry into the doctrine as it exists in England with an unwritten constitution and turn next to the twenty Latin-American nations to the south of us. There we find language in all of their constitutions which indicates their subscription to the doctrine of the separation of powers, with some of the constitutions being considerably more emphatic on the subject than others. For example, the constitutions of ten nations contain a strong statement to the effect that the exercise of the powers of government are entrusted to the legislative, executive and judicial branches which are to be separate and independent of each other,[66] although

---

[65] *La Réalisation de la Réforme Fiscale par la Voie Réglementaire;* Chornique, 1948 Recueil Dalloz 177, 178 (Paris, 1948).

[66] *Political Constitution of the Bolivian State,* Nov. 23, 1945 (as amended), reprinted in I Peaslee, *Constitutions of Nations* 153-176 (Concord, 1950), Art. 2; *Constitution of the United States of Brazil,* Sept. 24, 1946, reprinted in Peaslee, *id.,* 181–226, Art. 36; *Political Constitution of the Republic of Colombia,* Feb. 16, 1945, reprinted in Peaslee, *id.,* 469–498, Art. 55; *Political Constitution of Costa Rica,* Dec. 7, 1871 (as amended), reprinted in Peaslee, *id.,* 503–522, Art. 13; *Constitution of the Dominican Republic,*

in five of these ten countries there are additional constitutional
provisions to the effect that the three branches, while separate and
independent, are to "collaborate harmoniously." [67] The constitutions of the remaining ten Latin-American nations do not include
any specific provision for the separation of governmental powers,
yet the doctrine is tacitly recognized by the classic division of the
powers and functions of government among the legislative, executive and judicial branches as in our own Federal Constitution.[68]

Jan. 10, 1949, reprinted in Peaslee, *id.*, 658–676, Art. 2; *Constitution of El
Salvador,* Aug. 13, 1886 (as amended), reprinted in Peaslee, *id.*, 740–764,
Art. 4; *Constitution of the Republic of Haiti,* Nov. 22, 1946, reprinted in
Peaslee, *id.*, II, 112–130, Arts. 35, 36; *Political Constitution of the Republic
of Honduras,* March 28, 1936, reprinted in Peaslee, *id.*, 135-157, Art. 86;
Constitution of the Republic of Nicaragua, Jan. 21, 1948, reprinted in Peas-
lee, *id.*, 636-670, Arts. 9, 10; *Constitution of the Republic of Panama,*
March 1, 1946, reprinted in Peaslee, *id.*, 702–740, Art. 2.

[67] *Bolivian Const., id.,* Art. 2; *Brazilian Const., id.,* Art. 36; *Colombian
Const., id.,* Art. 55; *Nicaraguan Const., id.,* Art. 10; *Panamanian Const., id.,*
Art. 2.

[68] *Constitution of the Argentine Republic,* March 16, 1949, reprinted in
I Peaslee, *op. cit.,* 63-82, Arts. 41, 75, 89; *Constitution of the Republic of
Cuba,* July 5, 1940, reprinted in Peaslee, *id.,* 526–594, Art. 118; *Constitution
of the Republic of Ecuador,* Dec. 31, 1946, reprinted in Peaslee, *id.,* 680–716,
Arts. 26, 81, 113 (The Ecuador constitution, however, sets up a Council of
State with various functions which are executive, legislative and judicial in
nature, Arts. 145, 146); *Constitution of the Republic of Guatemala,* March
11, 1945, reprinted in Peaslee, *id.,* II, 71–107, Art. 2; *Political Constitution of
the United States of Mexico,* Jan. 31, 1917, reprinted in Peaslee, *id.,* 415–459,
Art. 49 (There is, however, strong language in the Mexican constitution
against unitary control in any one person: "The supreme power of the
federation is divided for its exercise into legislative, executive, and judicial.
Two or more of these powers shall never be united in one person or corporation, nor shall the legislative power be vested in one individual except in
the case of extraordinary powers granted to the executive, in accordance with
the provisions of Article 29. In no other case shall extraordinary powers
be granted to the executive to legislate." Art. 49.); *Constitution of the Republic of Peru,* April 9, 1933, reprinted in Peaslee, *id.,* 765–788, Pts. V, VII,

There are, moreover, provisions in various of the Latin- American constitutions specifically implementing the principle of the separation of powers. Thus there are constitutional prohibitions restraining the executive from exercising the functions of or infringing on the judiciary,[69] and from trespassing on the domain of the legislature,[70] while similar provisions prohibit the legislature from usurping the powers of either the judiciary[71] or the executive.[72] Nor is the judiciary without its special limitations, for a number of their constitutions declare that the function of a

XIII; *Constitution of the Oriental Republic of Uruguay,* March 24, 1934 (as amended Nov. 29, 1942), reprinted in Peaslee, *id.,* III, 391–430, Arts. 73, 145, 206; *Constitution of Venezuela,* July 5, 1947, reprinted in Peaslee, *id.,* 469–514, Art. 137, which recites that "Each one of the branches of the national power shall have its own functions; nevertheless, the bodies carrying out each power shall collaborate among themselves, and with the other public powers in the realization of the purposes of the state."

The Republics of Chile and Paraguay have the threefold division, although they do not use the classic designations. Thus Chile sets up a National Congress, a President of the Republic, and a judicial power. *Political Constitution of the Republic of Chile,* Sept. 18, 1925 (as amended), reprinted in I Peaslee, *id.,* 412-435, chaps. IV, V, VII. Paraguay provides for an executive power, a Chamber of Representatives, and a judicial power. *Constitution of the Republic of Paraguay,* July 10, 1940, reprinted in Peaslee, *id.,* II, 745–760, Arts. 45, 67, 80 (Note that the constitution also creates a Council of State with various powers mostly of a legislative nature. Arts. 62–66).

[69] *Argentine Const., op. cit.,* Art. 90; *Brazilian Const., op. cit.,* Art. 89, II; *Chilean Const., op cit.,* Art. 80; *Costa Rican Const., op. cit.,* Art 110(5); *Cuban Const., op. cit.,* Art. 122(a); *Ecuadorian Const., op. cit.,* Art. 98(3); *Paraguayan Const., op. cit.,* Art 87.

[70] *Brazilian Const., id.,* Art. 89, II; *Costa Rican Const., id.,* Art. 110(3); *Cuban Const., id.,* Art. 122(a); *Ecuadorian Const., id.,* Art. 98(4); *Peruvian Const., op. cit.,* Art. 150.

[71] *Chilean Const., op. cit.,* Art. 80; *Colombian Const., op. cit.,* Art. 78(2); *Ecuadorian Const., id.,* Art. 54(1).

[72] *Colombian Const., id.,* Art. 78(2); *Ecuadorian Const., id.,* Art. 54(1).

judge is incompatible with the exercise of other public powers, although usually he is permitted to hold teaching and academic positions, and occasionally assignments in the diplomatic service or on international courts and commissions are permitted.[73] Many Latin-American constitutions expressly empower the judiciary to interpret the constitution and to declare laws unconstitutional.[74] And in some of their constitutions may be found expressions to the effect that the whole of public power may not be concentrated in the executive or any other person, as well as restrictions on the legislature vesting the executive with extraordinary powers.[75]

In view of the wide variety of provisions purporting to espouse the separability of the functions of government, why is it that the doctrine of the separation of powers does not effectively operate in most Latin-American countries to prevent the concentration of power and the resultant deprivation of individual rights? The answer is not readily apparent. These countries have had a long history of revolts and revolutions which have resulted in the ascension to power of strong military leaders through means out-

[73] *Brazilian Const., op. cit.*, Art. 96; *Cuban Const., op. cit.*, Art. 207; *Dominican Republic Const., op. cit.*, Art. 60; *Ecuadorian Const., id.*, Art. 123; *Salvadoran Const., op. cit.*, Art. 106; *Guatemalan Const., op. cit.*, Art. 167; *Haitian Const., op. cit.*, Art. 105; *Mexican Const., op. cit.*, Art. 101; *Nicaraguan Const., op. cit.*, Art. 211; *Panamanian Const., op. cit.*, Art. 168; *Peruvian Const., op. cit.*, Art. 226; *Venezuelan Const., op. cit.*, Art. 217.

[74] *Argentine Const., op. cit.*, Art. 95; *Bolivian Const., op. cit.*, Art. 143-(5); *Brazilian Const., id.*, Art. 101, III; *Chilean Const., op. cit.*, Art. 86; *Colombian Const., op. cit.*, Art. 214; *Salvadoran Const., id.*, Art. 110; *Guatemalan Const., id.*, Art. 170; *Haitian Const., id.*, Art. 111; *Honduran Const., op. cit.*, Art. 145; *Mexican Const., id.*, Art. 105; *Nicaraguan Const., id.*, Arts. 213(17), 217; *Panamanian Const., id.*, Arts. 131, 167; *Peruvian Const., id.*, Art. 133; *Uruguayan Const., op. cit.*, Art. 229; *Venezuelan Const., id.*, Art. 220(7).

[75] *Argentine Const., id.*, Art. 20; *Bolivian Const., id.*, Art. 38; *Mexican Const., id.*, Art. 49; *Paraguayan Const., op. cit.*, Art. 16.

side the framework of the established government.[76] To protect the existing government against new revolutions it has generally been considered essential to grant to the executive great emergency powers. Whether or not the existence of these emergency powers has contributed to the stability of the governments in the Latin-American countries or has been a source of even greater instability is difficult to determine, but in any event the concentration of power in the executive and the obliteration of much of the significance of the doctrine of the separation of powers have long been a common political phenomenon in Latin America.

The constitutions of fifteen of these countries contain express provisions permitting the restriction or suspension of the ordinary constitutional guarantees during a period of emergency,[77] only five of their constitutions containing no specific provisions to this effect.[78] Moreover, a number of their constitutions contain provisions granting extraordinary powers in time of emergency to the legislature or chief executive.[79] Significantly there is general

[76] See Munroe, *The Latin American Republics, A History* (New York, 1950).

[77] *Argentine Const., op. cit.,* Art. 34; *Bolivian Const., op. cit.,* Art. 35(3); *Brazilian Const., op. cit.,* Art. 207; *Costa Rican Const., op. cit.,* Arts. 82(7), 109(3); *Cuban Const., op. cit.,* Art. 41; *Dominican Republic Const., op. cit.,* Art. 33(7, 8); *Salvadoran Const., op. cit.,* Art. 39; *Guatemalan Const., op. cit.,* Arts. 54, 138; *Haitian Const., op. cit.,* Art. 142; *Honduran Const., op. cit.,* Art. 83; *Mexican Const., op. cit.,* Art. 29; *Nicaraguan Const., op. cit.,* Art. 184; *Panamanian Const., op. cit.,* Art. 52; *Peruvian Const., op. cit.,* Art. 70; *Venezuelan Const., op. cit.,* Art. 76.

[78] *Chilean Const., op. cit.,* Art. 72(17); *Colombian Const., op. cit.,* Art. 121; *Ecuadorian Const., op. cit.,* Art. 94; *Paraguayan Const., op. cit.,* Art. 52; *Uruguayan Const., op. cit.,* Art. 157(18).

[79] *Bolivian Const., op. cit.,* Art. 35; *Brazilian Const., op. cit.,* Art. 209; *Colombian Const., id.,* Art. 121; *Cuban Const., op. cit.,* Arts. 281, 282; *Ecuadorian Const., id.,* Art. 94; *Mexican Const., op. cit.,* Art. 29; *Venezuelan Const., op. cit.,* Art. 198(18).

agreement in the Latin-American countries as to what justifies the taking of emergency action: almost without exception internal disorder or commotion, civil war, international war and an invasion by a foreign sovereign are considered adequate.[80]

The granting of extraordinary powers to the executive for the purpose of dealing with emergencies seriously affects the utility of the doctrine of the separation of powers unless the declaration of the emergency is left to the legislative branch and unless the courts have the power—and exercise it—to enjoin the executive from acting in the absence of such a declaration and from taking action not reasonably necessary to cope with a declared emergency. Any nation must be capable of dealing with special conditions that present a threat to its very existence, but in providing the executive with the necessary emergency powers effective checks and restraints must be available, else the remedy in the long run may prove more dangerous than the disease.

It is to be noted that in only twelve of the twenty Latin-American countries is the legislative organ given the power, in the first instance, to decree an emergency[81] and in nine of these if the

[80] *Argentine Const., op. cit.*, Art. 34; *Bolivian Const., id.*, Art. 34; *Brazilian Const., id.*, Art. 206; *Chilean Const., op. cit.*, Art. 72(17); *Colombian Const., id.*, Art. 121; *Costa Rican Const., op. cit.*, Art. 82(7); *Ecuadorian Const., id.*, Art. 94; *Guatemalan Const., op. cit.*, Art. 138; *Haitian Const., op. cit.*, Art. 142; *Honduran Const., op. cit.*, Art. 83; *Mexican Const., id.*, Art. 29; *Nicaraguan Const., op. cit.*, Art. 184; *Panamanian Const., op. cit.*, Art. 52; *Paraguayan Const., op. cit.*, Art. 52; *Uruguayan Const., op. cit.*, Art. 157(18); *Venezuelan Const., id.*, Art. 76. See also *Salvadoran Const., op. cit.*, Art. 68(23) (as determined by a special constitutional law); *Peruvian Const., op. cit.*, Art. 70 (when necessary for security of the nation); *Dominican Republic Const., op. cit.*, Art. 33(7, 8) (breach of public peace or national sovereignty is in grave and imminent danger).

[81] *Argentine Const., op. cit.*, Art. 68(25); *Brazilian Const., op. cit.*, Art. 206; *Chilean Const., op. cit.*, Art. 72(17); *Costa Rican Const., op. cit.*, Art.

legislature is in recess the president has the power to declare an emergency,[82] subject in five countries to ratification or invalidation by a special session of the legislature that must be called [83] and in four to approval or disapproval by the next regular session of the legislature.[84] In thirteen Latin-American nations the power to declare an emergency, even when the legislature is in session, rests with the executive.[85] The apparent overlapping in these figures is attributable to the fact that in five countries some kinds of emergencies may be declared by the legislature and others by the executive.[86]

82(7); *Cuban Const., op. cit.,* Arts. 41, 281, 282; *Dominican Republic Const., op. cit.,* Art 33(7, 8); *Ecuadorian Const., op. cit.,* Art. 94; *Salvadoran Const., op. cit.,* Art. 68(23); *Honduran Const., op. cit.,* Arts. 84, 101(20); *Nicaraguan Const., op. cit.,* Art. 133(5); *Panamanian Const., op. cit.,* Art. 53; *Venezuelan Const., op. cit.,* Art. 162(2).

[82] *Argentine Const., id.,* Art. 68(25); *Brazilian Const., id.,* Arts. 208, 211; *Chilean Const., id.,* Art. 72(17); *Costa Rican Const., id.,* Art. 109(3); *Cuban Const., id.,* Art. 41; *Dominican Republic Const., id.,* Arts. 33(8), 49 (8); *Salvadoran Const., id.,* Art. 91(16); *Honduran Const., id.,* Art. 84; *Panamanian Const., id.,* Art. 53.

[83] *Brazilian Const., op. cit.,* Arts. 208, 211; *Costa Rican Const., op. cit.,* Art. 109(3); *Cuban Const., op. cit.,* Art. 41; *Dominican Republic Const., op. cit.,* Arts. 33(8), 49(8); *Panamanian Const., op. cit.* Art. 53.

[84] *Argentine Const., op. cit.,* Art. 68(25); *Salavadoran Const., op. cit.,* Art. 91(16); *Chilean Const., op. cit.,* Art. 72(17); *Honduran Const., op. cit.,* Art. 84.

[85] *Bolivian Const., op. cit.,* Art. 34; *Colombian Const., op. cit.,* Art. 121; *Chilean Const., id.,* Art. 72(17); *Cuban Const., op. cit.,* Art. 41; *Ecuadorian Const., op. cit.,* Art. 95; *Guatemalan Const., op. cit.,* Art. 138; *Haitian Const., op. cit.,* Art. 142; *Mexican Const., op. cit.,* Art. 29; *Nicaraguan Const., op. cit.,* Art. 184; *Paraguayan Const., op. cit.,* Art. 52; *Peruvian Const., op. cit.,* Art. 70; *Uruguayan Const., op. cit.,* Art 157(18); *Venezuelan Const., op. cit.,* Arts. 76, 77.

[86] *Chilean Const., id.,* Art. 72(17) (legislature acts in case of internal disorder, executive in case of foreign attack); *Cuban Const., id.,* Art. 41 (either legislature or executive may act to suspend guarantees); *Ecuadorian*

The different Latin-American constitutions vary with respect
to the duration of the period of emergency which may be declared.
Some prescribe a 30-day limit subject to extension,[87] others 45
days, [88] 60 days, [89] and 90 days,[90] while in still others the limitation is expressed in such ambiguous terms as "a limited time," [91]
"temporarily suspended," [92] "for a determined period," [93] "the
duration," [94] "until the war is over or uprising suppressed," [95] "as
set forth in the decree," [96] or "as provided by law," [97] and a number of their constitutions place no limitation on the duration of
the emergency.[98]

Const., id., Arts 94, 95 (executive may act without applying to legislature
only in case of catastrophe); Nicaraguan Const., id., Arts. 133(5), 184
(legislature decrees economic emergency, executive acts to restrict constitutional guarantees); Venezuelan Const., id., Arts. 162(2), 76, 77 (legislature
decrees state of emergency, president may restrict constitutional guarantees).

[87] Brazilian Const., op. cit., Art. 210; Guatemalan Const., op. cit., Art.
138; Peruvian Const., op. cit., Art. 70.

[88] Cuban Const., op. cit., Arts. 41, 281.

[89] Costa Rican Const., op. cit., Art. 82(7); Honduran Const., op. cit.,
Art. 84; Venezuelan Const., op. cit., Art. 77 (refers to detention powers of
president).

[90] Bolivian Const., op. cit., Art. 34.

[91] Argentine Const., op. cit., Art. 83(19).

[92] Panamanian Const., op. cit., Art. 53.

[93] Chilean Const., op. cit., Art. 72(17).

[94] Dominican Republic Const., op. cit., Art. 33(7).

[95] Colombian Const., op. cit., Art. 121. See also Bolivian Const., id.,
Art. 34 and Brazilian Const., id., Art. 210 (both noting exception in case of
war as to duration of emergency).

[96] Ecuadorian Const., op. cit., Art. 96; Nicaraguan Const., op. cit., Art.
133(5) (as to economic emergency).

[97] Salvadoran Const., op. cit., Art. 68(23).

[98] Haitian Const., op. cit., Arts. 142, 143; Mexican Const., op. cit., Art.
29; Nicaraguan Const., op. cit., Art. 184 (as to suspension of constitutional

Generally the consequences of emergency action in the Latin-American countries are much more drastic than those we are accustomed to here. In most of these countries the immediate effect of an emergency decree is the suspension of all constitutional guarantees pertaining to civil liberties.[99] In some of them all guarantees (with occasional exceptions) in the geographical area where emergency action is taken are suspended by the decreeing of the emergency,[100] while in others only certain specified guarantees may be suspended.[101] In addition some of their constitutions provide for the exercise of special powers by the president during the emergency period.[102] Only a few constitutions declare that

guarantees); *Paraguayan Const., op. cit.,* Art. 52; *Uruguayan Const., op. cit.,* Art. 157(18); *Venezuelan Const., op. cit.,* Arts. 76, 162(2) (as to suspension of guarantees and as to state of emergency).

[99] *Argentine Const., op. cit.,* Art. 34; *Bolivian Const., op. cit.,* Art. 35 (3); *Brazilian Const., op. cit.,* Art. 207; *Costa Rican Const., op. cit.,* Arts. 82(7), 109(3); *Cuban Const., op. cit.,* Art. 41; *Dominican Republic Const., op. cit.,* Art. 33(7, 8); *Salvadoran Const., op. cit.,* Art. 39; *Guatemalan Const., op. cit.,* Arts. 54, 138; *Haitian Const., id.,* Art. 142; *Honduran Const., op. cit.,* Art. 83; *Mexican Const., id.,* Art. 29; *Nicaraguan Const., id.,* Art. 184; *Panamanian Const., op. cit.,* Art. 52; *Peruvian Const., op. cit.,* Art 70; *Venezuelan Const., id.,* Art. 76.

[100] *Argentine Const., id.,* Art. 34; *Haitian Const., id.,* Art. 142; *Mexican Const., id.,* Art. 29; *Nicaraguan Const., id.,* Art. 184; *Venezuelan Const., id.,* Art. 76.

[101] *Costa Rican Const., op. cit.,* Arts. 82(7), 109(3); *Cuban Const., op. cit.,* Art. 41; *Dominican Republic Const., op. cit.,* Art. 33(7, 8); *Guatemalan Const., op. cit.,* Arts. 54, 138; *Honduran Const., op. cit.,* Art. 83; *Panamanian Const., op. cit.,* Art. 52; *Peruvian Const., op. cit.,* Art. 70. See also *Brazilian Const., op. cit.,* Art. 207 (emergency decree specifies which guarantees remain in effect); *Bolivian Const., op. cit.,* Art. 35(3) (guarantees suspended as to individuals charged with conspiracy); *Salvadoran Const., op. cit.,* Art. 39 (law on the state of seige determines which guarantees will be suspended).

[102] *Bolivian Const., id.,* Art. 35; *Brazilian Const., id.,* Art. 209; *Colombian Const., op. cit.,* Art. 121; *Cuban Const., id.,* Art. 281, 282; *Ecuadorian*

the emergency status shall not affect the functioning of the public organs of government[103] with some specifically noting the retention by the legislators of their congressional immunities and prerogatives during the emergency.[104]

Aside from the provisions calling for ratification of executive action by the legislature, or requiring the executive to report and account to it, there are other provisions in various Latin-American constitutions which purport to put some restraint on executive action. The large majority of these restrictions, however, provide for a check on the executive only after the emergency has been declared and afford a remedy to those aggrieved only after the emergency is over. Thus, for example, in a number of their constitutions we find provisions declaring that the executive authority will be held accountable for any abuses committed during the emergency period,[105] but only three countries permit resort to the courts during the emergency period to check abuses.[106]

The extraordinary legislative powers of the executive are not confined to emergencies in many Latin-American countries. We are told by Rafael Bielsa, the eminent Argentine authority, that

Const., op. cit., Art. 94; Mexican Const., op. cit., Art. 29; Venezuelan Const., op. cit., Art. 198(18).

[103] Guatemalan Const., op. cit., Art. 138; Nicaraguan Const., op. cit., Art. 184; Venezuelan Const., id., Art. 78.

[104] Bolivian Const., op. cit., Art. 38; Brazilian Const., op. cit., Art. 213; Chilean Const., op. cit., Art. 72(17); Guatemalan Const., id., Art. 138; Honduran Const., op. cit., Art. 98(1); Nicaraguan Const., id., Art. 184; Venezuelan Const., id., Art. 78.

[105] Bolivian Const., id., Art. 35(4); Colombian Const., op. cit., Art. 121; Ecuadorian Const., op. cit., Art. 96; Salvadoran Const., op. cit., Art. 91(16); Guatemalan Const., id., Art. 139; Nicaraguan Const., id., Art. 184. See also Cuban Const., op. cit., Art. 282 (certain judicial acts can be reviewed after emergency).

[106] Brazilian Const., op. cit., Art. 215; Honduran Const., op. cit., Art. 85; Venezuelan Const., op. cit., Art. 77 (refers to detention powers of president).

the Latin-American executive, like the French premier, has the legislative power to promulgate such regulations as may be "necessary for the execution of the laws of the nation, taking care not to alter their spirit by regulatory exceptions." [107] This regulatory power, Bielsa says,

> consists partially in arranging commandments or principles of the law in particular precepts which are more analytical and precise with respect to the administrative activity, and necessary for their better and more successful application, and partly in defining, clarifying and interpreting—for the purpose of its better understanding and also of its popularization—the purpose of the law, i. e., of its more general principles, and to provide for specific norms for the execution of its commandments.

> ... ; this is precisely the purpose of the regulation; to make the administrative law more *specific and workable*.[108]

As under the Weimar Constitution in Germany, this executive power of the Latin-American president to issue regulations naturally tends to the issuance of emergency decrees. As Bielsa puts it:

> Nevertheless, the executive authorities by issuing regulations and general resolutions may invade the legislative sphere in a special and urgent case; it is then the question of norms which in principle only the legislator can establish, but the state of "emergency" and the operation of an essential purpose of the state requires that the authorities that provide for the realization of these purposes, without interruption of the continuity of its exercise, establish a norm by an act which for its special character is called *decree-law* (hybrid expression in a certain sense); the subsequent approval by Congress gives to this act

[107] I Bielsa, *Administrative Law and Science* 304 *et seq.* (2d ed. Buenos Aires, 1929).
[108] *Id.*

the character and force of law. Therefore, it must be held that a regulation of such a nature, even though precarious, is a relatively autonomous regulation, inasmuch as it is not sub-ordinated to any law although it is subject to the constitution and to the general principles of law. The executive authorities do not intend to substitute themselves for the legislator except for the purpose of providing for a function belonging to the executive, and to comply with a duty to the State.[109]

In the light of the constitutional provisions of the Latin-American countries it is inevitable that executive dominance is a far more common and more far-reaching phenomenon in those countries during times of crises than it has proved to be in the United States. In the Latin-American countries there have been more than a hundred revolutions since 1900 and innumerable re-volts.[110] While one may not assert a direct causal connection be-tween the framework of their constitutions and revolutions, it is obvious that the constitutional grant of emergency powers to the president and his frequent exercise of such powers, often in dic-tatorial fashion, does not make for respect for the constitutional rights of the individual. To an indeterminable extent therefore their constitutional deficiencies are an incitement to revolution and revolt.

It does not require much political acumen to perceive that in Russia, where the judgments of the courts may be set aside by an executive body, or in Hitler's Germany where the executive could by decree take over all government and even change the constitu-tion itself, or in a number of the countries of Latin America where the executive may almost at will declare an emergency and thus assume unlimited power, there is no such thing as individual

[109] *Id.*
[110] See Munroe, *op. cit.*

liberty and there cannot be a stable, progressive society. And even in France, whose republican institutions are in so many ways similar to our own, the executive is still exercising legislative power in flat defiance of the plain words of the Constitution and there is no court that will even hear a protest against such conduct. I am not suggesting that strict adherence to our doctrine of the separation of powers would have guaranteed to the individual the liberty that brave men in all of these lands have struggled for, but surely it must be conceded that the failure to have provided in the organic law against unwarranted interference with both the fundamental rights of the individual and the stability of the normal processes of government indicates a fundamental lack of perception of the nature of the relationship that must exist between the citizen and the state if the rights of both the individual and society are to be assured. Is there any more depressing fact in the whole catalogue of the world's woes today than this tragic lack of understanding in so many quarters, first, of the relation between the separation of powers and the rule of law and, second, of the relation between the rule of law, as a substitute for force and tyranny, and individual freedom and the dignity of man? Particularly is this so when the world over restlessness, discontent and revolution predominate without, however, there being any clear comprehension of the desired goals or the way of obtaining them.

The world has not experienced such times since the revolutionary period of about a century ago. Indeed, we have to go back to the era of the American Revolution, the French Revolution, and the English Industrial Revolution of a century and three quarters ago for a close parallel. In that era mankind added political freedom and some measure of economic freedom to the intellectual and religious freedom it had achieved in earlier centuries. In recent decades, however, we have been so absorbed in scientific research and in the development of technology that we have quite neglected the ever-increasing problems of government. In the last half century medical skill and scientific discoveries have added eighteen years to our normal life expectancy and have made every moment of it more comfortable. The automobile and the airplane, the radio and television have brought us thrills and enjoyment—and problems—unknown in the 1800's. Inventions and discoveries in the physical sciences have come at such a pace that textbooks in these fields are outmoded almost before they are off the printing press. Within the past few weeks we have read of an inexpensive drug that promises a cure for tuberculosis and of a simple process for converting salt water into fresh thereby making it possible to use sea water for irrigation. In all, two billion dollars a year are spent in this country on scientific research and with marvelous results, yet the field of law and government remains quite neglected, even though with our forty-eight sovereign states we have the best available political laboratories in the world.

Is not the greatest danger to the whole world that, in our preoccupation with natural science and technology and with all the comforts and enjoyment they afford us, we and the world as well may lose all for want of an understanding or, worse yet, for lack of any interest in the fundamental political processes of governing ourselves in such a way as to insure the maintenance of essential human rights in a strong, progressive society? To be more specific, is it not alarming that in a country such as ours only 59% of the eligible voters should have cast their vote for a presidential candidate in 1940, only 56% in 1944, and merely 51% in 1948? Compare these figures, if you will, with the 70% that voted here in the presidential election in 1900, with the 93% that voted in Italy in 1948, and with the 95% that voted in free Austria in 1949. Furthermore, how many of our present-day voters are well informed and actuated solely by regard for the best interests of the country as a whole? Will 1952 find only a minority of the voters going to the polls to vote for a president? Will he be selected for this post of transcendent importance in the world today solely on the basis of his merits? Even the best form of government cannot survive public apathy or selfishness.

Right-thinking men have never had much difficulty in formulating the grand objective of good government—the maximum of individual freedom consistent, first, with a like freedom for every other individual and, second, with a stable, yet progressive society. Only thus can society attain its greatest effectiveness and the individual full usefulness and happiness. The objective has been clearly stated in varying phrases hundreds or thousands of times but never better than by Heraclitus of Ephesus 2500 years ago:

> The major problem of human society is to combine that degree of liberty without which law is tyranny with that degree of law without which liberty becomes license.

The great difficulties have always been, first, to discover the practical means of achieving the grand objective and, second, to find the opportunity for applying these means in the ever-shifting tangle of human affairs. A large part of man's effort over the centuries has been expended in seeking a solution of these great problems. Whenever opportunity has afforded, mankind has instinctively sought to substitute a reign of law for official whim, no matter how beneficent. Men have known from sad experience centuries before Lord Acton said it, that "Power tends to corrupt, and absolute power corrupts absolutely." [111] A reign of law, in contrast to the tyranny of power, may be achieved only through separating appropriately the several powers of government.

[111] *Essays on Freedom and Power* 364 (Boston, 1948).

Our doctrine of the separation of powers has a long history running over centuries, but we can trace it merely in barest outline. First of all, we owe much to the efforts of the political philosophers in their search for the secret of good government. Plato compromised the ideals he had set forth in *The Republic* and advocated, for purposes of practical stability, a "mixed state"[112] in which he expected to temper the oligarchical tendency of the nobility with the democratic institution of choice by lot and to restrain the rule of the *demos* with qualities such as virtue and wisdom which were then considered the attributes of the aristocrats.[113] "This principle," says Sabine, "is the ancestor of the famous separation of powers which Montesquieu was to rediscover centuries later as the essence of the political wisdom embodied in the English constitution."[114] Aristotle, as did Plato, left off speculating as to the best possible form of government and accepted Plato's mixed state as the only expedient for insuring a stable, lasting government. It was his thesis that since the state existed for the "sake of a good life," those "who contribute[d] most to such a society [should] have a greater share in it."[115] However, since each class contributed positive values of its own,[116] he found his solution in a blend of oligarchy and democracy with the middle class serving as a buffer between the rich and the poor.[117] Aristotle saw three levels or elements of political func-

[112] In his *Statesman* and more especially in his *Laws,* the Jowett translation, II *The Dialogues of Plato* (Random House ed., New York, 1937).

[113] *Laws, id.,* Bk. VI, 757.

[114] Sabine, *A History of Political Theory* 79 (New York, rev. ed. 1950).

[115] *Politics,* Bk. III, 1280a, 31–32; 1281a, 4–5, the Jowett translation in *Basic Works of Aristotle* (McKeon-Random House ed., New York, 1941).

[116] *Id.,* Bk. III, 1283a, 40–1286a, 34; 1283b, 13–34; 1286b, 22–25; 1287a, 10–30; 1287b, 40–1288a, 33.

[117] *Id.,* Bk. IV, 1293b, 33–34; 1296b, 40–1297a, 8.

tions: the deliberative, the magisterial and the judicative[118]—which has led many to regard him as the originator of the doctrine of separation of powers.[119] This, it is submitted, is a misconception, since he was merely describing the functions necessarily exercised by the sovereign body however constituted. He laid no stress on whether they should be separated in their operation. While Aristotle and Plato sought stability by blending the forces of the several classes within society, Polybius thought he had found stability in the Roman constitution in "a reciprocal antagonism of organs." [120] Polybius thought that the major political organs of the government should be representative of the different classes, and in the resulting competition each organ would act as a balance and check against the others.[121]

Between these early philosophers and those who came after the middle ages, there is a chasm greater than that of mere time. Man as a political fraction of the state gave way to man as an individual, and as against the goal of stability in government there arose that new concept, the freedom of a people to control its own destiny. This change so permeated the philosophical structure of the time that Marsilius de Padua, one of the foremost

[118] *Id.*, Bk. IV, 1297b, 35–1301a, 16.

[119] See for examples Bondy, *The Separation of Governmental Powers,* 5 Col. Univ. Studies in Hist., Eco., and Pub. Law 139, 144 (New York, 1896); Fairlie, *The Separation of Powers,* 21 Mich. L. Rev. 393 (1923); Garner, *Introduction to Political Science* 411 (New York, 1910). See also Frankfurter and Davison, *Cases and Materials on Administrative Law* (2d ed., Chicago, 1935) where in the Introduction excerpts from Aristotle, Locke and Montesquieu follow in that order to show the origins of the separation of powers doctrine.

[120] Dunning, *A History of Political Theories, Ancient and Medieval* 118 (New York, 1902).

[121] Sabine, *op. cit.,* 154–155; see also Dunning, *Ancient and Medieval, op. cit.,* 113–118.

medieval philosophers, denied the tenet so fundamental with Plato and Aristotle that the function of good government was the inculcation of moral virtue. Rather he found the function to be the adjudication of disputes and the punishment of crimes.[122] Since he believed the trustworthiness and intelligence of the people as a whole superior to that of any one of its classes, he had no use for the theory of the mixed state.[123] He did, however, distinguish between the function of legislating, which he believed best done by the entire people as an expression of their collective will, and the function of executing law, which included tasks we would call adjudicative as well as executive.[124] This distribution of functions was utilitarian rather than political in purpose,[125] however, as was that of Jean Bodin two centuries later. Like Marsilius, Bodin saw no value in "mixed government." [126] It was his conclusion that the sovereign power that determined the existence of a state was a unity; hence "mixed government" could be nothing but anarchy. In the surge of national determinism that marked the Renaissance, Bodin wrote to support the monarchy where the unity he thought necessary for sovereign power was an actuality. He reasoned, however, that wherever the ultimate authority in government was decided to rest, it was possible to have a mixed administration.[127] In the administration of the state Bodin felt that it was wise, but not necessary, to have a senate to advise the

[122] This was in his major opus, the *Defensor Pacis,* written in 1324. The standard translation is that of Previte-Orton (Cambridge, 1928), but Gewirth will shortly publish a new one as the second volume of a critical study of the work of Marsilius. See I Gewirth, *Marsilius of Padua* 136-147 (New York, 1951).

[123] Gewirth, *op. cit.,* 203–225, 240–241, 246–247.

[124] *Id.,* 229–232.

[125] *Id.,* 235.

[126] His *Six Livres de la République* was published in 1576.

[127] See Sabine, *op. cit.,* c XX; Dunning, *A History of Political Theories*

sovereign on the enactment of law and that it was essential to have a separate, though not independent, judiciary. Thus he saw the desirability of a functional separation within a framework of centralized power.[128]

But even while Bodin in France and Hobbes in England were busy building the case for absolutism, there had begun a great flood of protests in the name of individual liberty. Bodin himself had been touched by this when he refused to his absolute sovereign the right over the property of his subjects.[129] The antimonarchists all traced ultimate sovereignty to the people who by contract, they maintained, empowered the king as ruler. The king was bound by his contract and responsible to the people who could resist or depose him if he contravened the natural law. This was the theory espoused, among others, by James Harrington.[130] The difficulty, of course, was to keep the ruler responsive to his subjects, at least those of his subjects who were landed and thus held political power;[131] and Harrington for this purpose suggested rotation in office, a secret ballot and a combination of mixed government and separation of functions.[132] Harrington, insofar as he saw only two governmental functions, the making and executing of law, followed Marsilius and Bodin; but insofar

From Luther to Montesquieu c. III (New York, 1905). The latter will henceforth be cited as "Dunning, Luther to Montesquieu."

[128] See especially Baudrillart, J. Bodin et Son Temps 310–323 (Paris, 1853). See also Allen, A History of Political Thought in the Sixteenth Century pt. 3, c. VII (3d ed., London, 1951); Sabine, op. cit., c. XX Dunning, Luther to Montesquieu, op. cit., c. III.

[129] Allen, op. cit., 422.

[130] The Commonwealth of Oceana in The Oceana and Other Works (Toland ed., London, 1700).

[131] Id., 39.

[132] Sabine, op. cit., 504.

as he advocated the checks and balances of mixed government he was reflecting the development in English government. Although he saw but two functions, Harrington saw three organs: "the Senate proposing, the People resolving, and the Magistracy executing; whereby partaking of Aristocracy . . . Democracy . . . and Monarchy." [133] There is no provision in his plan, however, for a judiciary apart from the executive. Writing in the middle of the seventeenth century at the same time as Harrington, Marchamont Nedham accorded the judiciary the same cavalier treatment.[134] Nedham favored popular rule and thus rejected the checks and balances of mixed government, finding sufficient security in education, rotation in office, and the separation of the legislative and executive functions, the latter including the judicial.[135] Concerning this separation he warned that "if the law-makers . . . should also be the constant administrators and dispensers of law and justice, then by consequence the people would be left without a remedy in case of injustice since no appeal can lie under heaven against such as have supremacy." [136] While both Nedham and Harrington were preparing the ground for their more illustrious successors, they were themselves still closer to the utilitarian than to the political separation of powers: in both their schemes the executive was elected and empowered by the legislature.[137] Locke agreed with these precursors of ministerial government. He wrote

[133] Harrington, *op. cit.*, 48, 59. See also his *Political Aphorisms,* Nos. 74–77 in the same collection of works, 519.

[134] *Excellencie of a Free State,* published originally in 1656.

[135] Gooch, *English Democratic Ideas in the Seventeenth Century* 160–162 (2d ed. rev. and supplemented by Laski, Cambridge, 1927).

[136] As quoted by 3 Adams, *Defense of the Constitutions of Government of the United States* c. II in 6 *Works of John Adams* 170 (Adams ed., Boston, 1851).

[137] Harrington, *op. cit.,* 131–132; Nedham, in Adams, *id.,* 170–177.

in 1690 to justify the Glorious Revolution of 1688,[138] and his model of political organization was the one formed by the Convention Parliament. Basing his study on the social contract, Locke found the legislative power supreme.[139] It is true that he perceived two other powers: the executive power over internal affairs, and the federative or the executive power over external affairs, but he saw them as exercised by only one other organ, an organ moreover which was to exercise the judicial power as well.[140] He further followed the example before him by dividing the legislative power between the monarch and a two-chamber Parliament and by treating the executive as an agent of the legislature.[141] Moreover, what separation there was Locke justified not only on grounds of expediency in governmental management but also as essential for the maintenance of liberty.[142]

But in the age-old search of the political philosophers for the secret of sound government combined with individual liberty, it was Montesquieu who first saw the light. Montesquieu ranked with Voltaire and Rousseau as one of the great influences of the eighteenth century on public affairs, not only in France, but in Europe and America. No better example of his influence can be found than James Madison, the father of our Constitution. Madison studied Montesquieu's *The Spirit of Laws* in a postgraduate course at Princeton, and it has been said that his knowledge of it "was so accurate that twenty years after he had left Princeton he

[138] *Second Treatise of Civil Government* (Gough ed., Oxford, 1946).

[139] *Id.,* c. VIII, § 89, c. X, § 132.

[140] Locke, *op. cit.,* c. XII, §§ 144, 146, 147, 148.

[141] Esmein, *Elements de Droit Constitutionnel* 282–283 (Paris, 1896); Fridrich, *Constitutional Government and Democracy* 173 (Boston, 1941).

[142] Locke, *op. cit.,* c. XII, §§ 143–144.

could quote it freely from memory without errors." [143] Montesquieu aimed to state the sociological influences on the organization of government and to analyze the constitutional requisites for
the preservation of liberty. He, first among the political philosophers, saw the necessity of separating the judiciary from the
executive and legislative branches of government; but this was
hardly an invention, for when he wrote in 1748, the Act of Settlement (1701) had already guaranteed judicial tenure during good
behavior to the English judges. He was nevertheless the first to
conceive of the three functions of government as exercised by
three distinct organs, each juxtaposed against the others. This
scheme Montesquieu saw in the mixed government of England.[144]
He saw the executive as monarchic,[145] the bicameral legislature
as aristocratic and democratic,[146] and the judiciary, perhaps because it did not fit in with this scheme, as "next to nothing." [147]
By his threefold representation of classes he hoped to balance the
economic powers in society as by his threefold separation of
functions he hoped to balance the political.

Montesquieu believed that there could be no liberty without
the separation of functions:

> Here then is the fundamental constitution of the government
> we are treating of. The legislative body being composed of
> two parts, they check one another by the mutual privilege of

[143] Carpenter, *Political Education in the Time of John Witherspoon,*
28 Princeton Alumni Weekly 489 (1928).

[144] *Spirit of Laws* Bk XI, c. VI (pp. 173-186 in Vol. I of Nugent's
two-volume translation published by Robert Clarke, Cincinnati, 1873).

[145] *Id.,* par. 36 (p. 179 in I Nugent). Paragraph numbers have been
supplied for easier reference.

[146] *Id.,* pars. 30-32 (p. 178 in I Nugent).

[147] *Id.,* par. 32 (p. 178 in I Nugent).

·rejecting. They are both restrained by the executive power, as the executive is by the legislative.[148]

These three powers should naturally form a state of repose or inaction. But as there is a necessity for movement in the course of human affairs, they are forced to move, but still in concert.[149]

It is clear that Montesquieu never envisioned a complete separation of powers. He realized that the efficient operation of government involved a certain degree of overlapping and that the theory of checks and balances required each organ to impede too great an aggrandizement of authority by the other two powers.[150]

The influence of Montesquieu everywhere was tremendous. As Holdsworth says, "He convinced the world that he had discovered a new constitutional principle which was universally valid." It does not detract from Montesquieu's influence to say that in his distaste for Louis XIV and Richelieu and all their works he saw more perfection in England than actually existed there. As Lévy-Ullmann, a distinguished French authority on comparative law, puts it, "England and the English were to him but a misty vision as he gazed from his vineyard in sunlit Gascony, three hundred years after the battle of Castillon." [151] Montesquieu failed, among other things, to see the King's role in legislation, the dual position of the House of Lords as the high court and the upper branch of the legislature, and the beginnings of ministerial government which would lead in due season to the supremacy of Parliament.

---

[148] *Id.,* par. 55 (p. 183 in I Nugent).

[149] *Id.,* par. 56 (p. 183 in I Nugent).

[150] See for example *id.,* pars. 41, 44, 48-50, 52-53 (pp. 180-193 in I Nugent).

[151] *The English Legal Tradition* 234 (London, 1935) translated by Mitchell.

Nor did he discern that in local government the tripartite division of powers did not exist, that local governments obtained their powers from Parliament and that the courts through the prerogative writs held them along with all other subordinate jurisdictions within their proper sphere of activity. This supervisory power of the courts was well known to the early American lawyer and statesman, not only through Coke and Blackstone, but also through their colonial experience which was followed in the new states. The supervisory jurisdiction of the courts over local bodies helped pave the way for judicial review as to the constitutionality of legislation. Our forefathers were familiar with English constitutional history and they appreciated, in spite of their quarrels with the mother country, the superiority in terms of individual freedom of the English constitutional government of their day with its limited monarchy over the absolute monarchies of the Continent. They recognized Bracton's maxim "The King is below no man, but he is below God and the law" [152] as one of the foundations of English constitutional government, and they found in Sir Edward Coke's declaration that "Magna Charta is such a fellow that he will have no sovereign" [153] the basis for constitutional guaranteees of individual freedom. In a very real sense, then, English constitutional experience, quite apart from Montesquieu's formulation of it, entered into American thinking in the drafting of the federal and state constitutions and may be regarded as a second great source of the American doctrine of the separation of powers.

The third source of the doctrine, and the one closest to the daily life of the framers of the Federal Constitution, was the un-

---

[152] *De Legibus Et Consuetudinibus Angliae,* Folio 34, as edited by Woodbine, vol. 1, p. 124 (New Haven, 1915).

[153] From debate in House of Commons, May 17, 1628.

happy experience of the American colonists with King George III and his bureaucrats, particularly in the shape of royal governors in the colonies and of the Privy Council in England. The colonists deemed themselves English subjects with all the rights of Englishmen. They became convinced they were being unlawfully denied their rights by English officialdom and in this they were supported by a substantial body of English opinion led by such men as Chatham and Burke. Their grievances were epitomized in the eloquent charges of the Declaration of Independence and require no amplification here. Particularly were they aggrieved at the centralized control of the Privy Council over the colonies, resulting in the disallowance of colonial statutes, instructions to the royal governors, and a jealous insistence on hearing in England appeals from the colonial courts regardless of the amount involved. As colonists they had enough of a completely centralized government with no distribution of powers and they were intent on seeing to it that they should never suffer such grievances from a government of their own construction.

The fourth great source of the American doctrine of the separation of powers as embodied in the Federal Constitution was the hard common sense and political sagacity of the Founding Fathers in convention assembled. Madison had studied every previous attempt at federal government from the earliest times and was the recognized scholar of the Convention, but there were many others who were serious students of government and active practitioners of it. Their wealth of experience in practical statecraft is reflected in the checks and balances of the Constitution as debated in the Constitutional Convention [154] and expounded in the *Federalist Papers*.

[154] Farrand, *The Records of the Federal Convention of 1787* (New Haven, 1911).

Nor was the doctrine with its accompanying checks and balances the only device resorted to for curtailing governmental powers. The Founding Fathers were equally concerned with the proper distribution of governmental power between the nation and the several states as a means of preserving the nation on the one side and individual freedom on the other. Strong local government within each state, moreover, they took for granted from English constitutional history and their own colonial experience. Thus governmental powers were fractionalized both horizontally and vertically in a deliberate effort to avoid an undue concentration of powers at any one spot. Montesquieu recognized the importance of this principle as clearly as he did the significance of the separation of powers when he wrote:

> It is therefore very probable that mankind would have been at length obliged to live constantly under the government of a single person, had they not contrived a kind of constitution that has all the internal advantages of a republican, together with the external force of a monarchical, government. I mean a confederate republic.[155]

In 1789, although to some degree a seafaring folk, we were primarily an agricultural people. Now, although agriculture is still of tremendous importance, we are primarily a manufacturing nation and urban interests tend to predominate. For a century and a quarter, barring four minor wars which today would be deemed but skirmishes, we had only one intensive conflict, the Civil War. This striking contrast with European military experience has now disappeared. In the past third of a century we have been in three World Wars—I say three because in Korea we have already lost more men and spent more in armament than in any other American war except World War II. The mili-

[155] Montesquieu, *op. cit.*, Bk. IX, c. I, par. 3 (p. 145 in I Nugent).

tary has thus come, unexpectedly and unwanted, to have a dominant influence on our entire economic life. The last three quarters of a century, moreover, have been marked by the rise of big business with its tremendous aggregation of capital. This has been matched in turn by the economic influence of powerful nationwide labor unions. The concentration of great economic power in a relatively few large corporations and in large unions has been the subject of much concern to thoughtful men. This concentration has in turn led to increased growth of governmental authority. Meanwhile time and space have been shrinking. A resident of Englewood, New Jersey may now dial directly the telephone number of a friend in San Francisco. One may go to the theatre one evening in New York, enjoy a comfortable night's sleep on a plane and have breakfast in Los Angeles at eight o'clock the next morning. Even more significant than the shrinkage of time and space in this age of overorganization has been a sense of the shrinkage of the influence of the average individual. There has been a marked tendency to think of man merely as a cog in the economic machine. Happily, however, this tendency seems to have been checked, in part because of a postwar resurgence of interest in religion which is fostering a militant faith in the worth of the individual and of his capacity for good and in part because of our alarm over the spread of totalitarian government and its effect on the individual.

Like so many other principles in our law the doctrine of the separation of powers has had a varied history. In the period from 1789 down to the Civil War the Congress was clearly the predominant part of the national government as the legislatures were in most states. From the Civil War to the opening days of the twentieth century the courts, both federal and state, loomed large in the public eye. The outbreak of World War I marked the beginning of the hegemony of the executive branch of the government especially in the federal sphere. This same period was also marked by the expansion of the functions of the federal government at the expense of the state government and to some degree of the growth of state government at the expense of local government. But while one department of government after another has had its day in the sun, none has ever succeeded in completely displacing the others, nor will it so long as the Federal Constitution with its underlying premise of the supremacy of law is given practical effect in the courts.

The doctrine of the separation of governmental powers is not a mere theoretical, philosophical concept. It is a practical, workaday principle. The division of government into three branches does not imply, as its critics would have us think, three watertight compartments. Montesquieu, as we have seen, knew better; the three departments, he said, must move "in concert." [156] This view is generally accepted. Madison, writing in the *Federalist,* said:

> (I)t may clearly be inferred that, in saying, "There can be no liberty where the legislative and executive powers are united in the same person, or body of magistrates," or, "if the power of judging be not separated from the legislative and executive powers," he (Montesquieu) did not mean that these departments ought to have no *partial agency* in, or no *control* over, the acts of each other. His meaning, as his own words import, and still more conclusively as illustrated by the example in his eye, can amount to no more than this, that where the *whole* power of one department is exercised by the same hands which possess the *whole* power of another department, the fundamental principles of a free constitution are subverted.[157]

The contest between the three departments in national, state and

---

[156] *Id.,* Bk. XI, c. VI, par. 56 (p. 183 in I Nugent).
[157] *The Federalist No. 47,* op. cit., 314, 315.

local governments still goes on from day to day with varying results, but with all of the skirmishes, sometimes none too edifying, the goal remains constant—a government of law rather than of official will or whim. This goal can only be attained by a government of limited powers distributed both vertically and horizontally, as a glance at the dictatorships of today and yesterday will demonstrate to all who are willing to learn from the experience of others.

II

THE DOMINANCE OF THE FEDERAL GOVERN-MENT OVER THE STATES AND OF THE FEDERAL EXECUTIVE OVER THE LEGISLATIVE BRANCH AS A THREAT TO THE DOCTRINE AND TO CONSTITUTIONAL GOVERNMENT

THE overwhelming growth in size and power of the executive branch of the federal government in comparison with the other two great departments has been the outstanding American political phenomenon of the twentieth century. To some extent this growth has been paralleled in the states. Insofar as these movements parallel each other, they may be said to represent the inevitable result of government's assuming new functions in response to popular demands. The pattern is fairly uniform: the legislature passes a statute imposing obligations on the executive branch in some new field; the statute requires uniformity of administration throughout the state or the nation as the case may be; such uniformity in turn necessitates an increase in the activity of the central government; and this increased activity of the

central government calls for paid professional officials either re-
placing or supplementing local officials, often amateurs. This
centralization of responsibility also involves the delegation of
legislative power to these professional officials, because the legislature cannot foresee every phase of the particular complicated social
or economic problem under consideration; indeed, one great
reason why the legislature often delegates legislative authority to
the executive department is that it hopes the executive will be able
to find through experiment and experience the solution that the
legislature has not succeeded in discovering. Every such statute
and every regulation promulgated thereunder inevitably impinges
on the activities of the citizen and often on the functions of
government, generally at the local level but also in the case of
federal statutes on the functions of state government. The process necessarily leads to a bureaucratic attitude in government. In
an article on *The Limitations of the Expert,* Harold J. Laski, who
would never be considered a conservative, has described the char-
acteristics of the bureaucratic mind:

> Special knowledge and the highly trained mind produce their
> own limitations which, in the realm of statesmanship, are of
> decisive importance. *Expertise,* it may be argued, sacrifices
> the insight of common sense to intensity of experience. It
> breeds an inability to accept new views from the very depth
> of its preoccupation with its own conclusions. It too often fails
> to see round its subject. It sees its results out of perspective by
> making them the center of relevance to which all other results
> must be related. Too often, also, it lacks humility; and this
> breeds in its possessors a failure in proportion which makes
> them fail to see the obvious which is before their very noses.
> It has, also, a certain caste-spirit about it, so that experts
> tend to neglect all evidence which does not come from those
> who belong to their own ranks. Above all, perhaps, and this
> most urgently where human problems are concerned, the ex-

pert fails to see that every judgment he makes not purely factual in nature brings with it a scheme of values which has no special validity about it. He tends to confuse the importance of his facts with the importance of what he proposes to do about them.[1]

Laski is here describing the genuine expert. We can only conjecture what he would have to say of the official with whom we are all familiar whose only claim to expertness inheres in the fact that he holds public office. Even with respect to the true expert Laski sounds a warning which everyone interested in good government will do well to heed:

> We must ceaselessly remember that no body of experts is wise enough, or good enough, to be charged with the destiny of mankind. Just because they are experts, the whole of life is, for them, in constant danger of being sacrificed to a part; and they are saved from disaster only by the need of deference to the plain man's common sense.[2]

The process we have been describing, of legislative enactment followed by administrative rule-making, also involves investigation and adjudication by administrative officials, expert or otherwise. It is a process that has been repeated in scores of activities in every state and hundreds of times in the federal government. The collective effect of this process brings us face to face with one of the fundamental problems of government, which has never been better expressed than by a young French judge who visited America a century ago to study its institutions and found much to admire. Says Alexis de Tocqueville in his *Democracy in America*:

> Certain interests are common to all parts of a nation, such as the enactment of its general laws and the maintenance of its

[1] 162 *Harper's Magazine* 101, 102 (1950).
[2] *Id.*, 109.

foreign relations. Other interests are peculiar to certain parts of the nation, such, for instance, as the business of the several townships. When the power that directs the former or general interests is concentrated in one place or in the same persons, it constitutes a centralized government. To concentrate in like manner in one place the direction of the latter or local interests, constitutes what may be termed a centralized administration.

. . . I cannot conceive that a nation can live and prosper without a powerful centralization of government. But I am of the opinion that a centralized administration is fit only to enervate the nations in which it exists, by incessantly diminishing their local spirit. Although such an administration can bring together at a given moment, on a given point, all the disposable resources of a people, it injures the renewal of those resources. It may ensure a victory in the hour of strife, but it gradually relaxes the sinews of strength. It may help admirably the transient greatness of a man, but not the durable prosperity of a nation.[3]

Of the soundness of his reasoning then and now there can be no doubt. The problem is difficult, but it is not beyond solution. For example, in a modern judicial department five, seven or nine judges set the rules for the entire judiciary of a state or of the nation with but a minimum of interference in the individual judge's actual conduct of the mass of litigation. Cannot similar techniques be developed in the administrative field? May not many of the new tasks of government be performed at the local level by local officials? To the extent that this can be done, is it not obviously preferable to a centralized administration in either state or nation?

In the federal sphere, however, extraordinary forces have been working toward a far greater concentration of power in the execu-

[3] Vol. I, pp. 86-87 (Bradley ed., New York, 1946). The first part of de Tocqueville's great work was originally published in Paris in 1835 and the second part in 1840.

tive branch than we find in the states. The nationwide depression of the 1930s called for nationwide remedies. War can be waged only on a national basis and we have had three in less than half a century. As a result of these wars world leadership in international affairs has been thrust on us and it, too, can be carried on only on a national basis. And the financial burden that such leadership has come to entail in the topsy-turvy world can be met only on a national basis. But there are still many functions that the federal government has taken over, or desires to take over from the state or local government, either outright or through control by grants-in-aid, that could be exercised equally well or better by state or local governments had they the funds available —funds that now flow in a never-ceasing stream into the federal treasury by virtue of the Sixteenth Amendment and are largely expended under the "general welfare" clause without any judicial decision available on the propriety of such expenditures by reason of the unwillingness of the Supreme Court to pass on what is or is not in the general welfare.[4] So long as this situation continues and a great variety of legislation goes unchallenged because there is none with standing to challenge it, little can be done to return the federal government to its proper bounds and to restore that balance in government which the Constitution intended.[5]

It would be wearisome to catalog, item by item, the ever-increasing scope of the activities of the executive branch of government, state and federal, but the growth is reflected in the increase in public employment. In 1900 one out of every 24 workers was on a government payroll; in 1920, two years after World War I,

[4] *Massachusetts v. Mellon,* 262 U.S. 447 (1923). See concurring opinion of Mr. Justice Brandeis in *Ashwander v. Tennessee Valley Authority,* 297 U.S. 288, 346-348 (1936).

[5] See Field, *Separation and Delegation of Powers,* 41 Am. Pol. Sci. Rev. 1101, 1108 (1947).

one out of 15; in 1947, two years after World War II, one out of 11; and today one out of 9.[6] The federal government alone, according to the latest available summary, has 1,816 component parts divided into 9 departments, 104 bureaus, 12 sections, 108 services, 51 branches, 460 offices, 631 divisions, 19 administrations, 6 agencies, 16 areas, 40 boards, 6 commands, 20 commissions, 19 corporations, 5 groups, 10 headquarters, 20 units, 3 authorities, and 263 miscellaneous functionally designated parts.[7] Its growth in recent years can best be indicated by a few apt comparisons. In the ten years from 1940 to 1950 the number of federal civilian employees increased over 100%,[8] while the number of persons employed by all the state and local governments increased only 25%.[9] On January 1, 1952, the federal government employed 2½ million civilians, and their number is currently growing at the rate of over 500 a day.[10] It does not require much imagination to appreciate the economic, political and social effects of such mass governmental employment. The situation is the same in the armed forces. On VE Day with over 12 million men in uniform there were 397 generals and admirals in Washington; as of the end of last September with only 3½ million men in uniform— less than one third of the number available on VE Day—there

[6] Fabricant, *The Rising Trend of Government Employment* 5 (Nat. Bur. of Econ. Res., 1949); 38 Fed. Res. Bull. 438 (1952). The figures for 1900 and 1920 include persons in the armed forces, those for 1947 and 1949 do not.

[7] *Big Government: Can It Be Managed Efficiently?* Fortune Magazine, special supplement 4 (May, 1949).

[8] Bureau of the Census, *Statistical Abstract of the U. S. 1951*, 193, Table 222.

[9] *Id.*, 199, Table 232.

[10] Report on Personnel, Joint Committee on Reduction of Nonessential Federal Expenditures, 82d Cong., 2d Sess., Sen. Doc. No. 101 (1952).

were 361 generals and admirals in Washington. Said one Senate committee, "Unless this trend is halted we could wind up with the fighting forces composed of all chiefs and no Indians." [11] Speaking of Indians, there is one bureaucrat on the payroll of the Indian Affairs Bureau for every 30 Indians in the United States.[12]

In whatever direction we turn we find the federal government dwarfing state and local governments. For example, in 1930 the total revenue of all state and local governments was almost double the revenue of the federal government, but by 1950 the situation was completely reversed with the federal receipts more than double those of the state and local governments combined.[13] Governmental expenditures tell a similar story. In 1915, 53% of the total expenditures for government was made at the local level, 19% by the states and only 28% by the federal government. By 1940 the expenditures of the federal government exceeded the combined expenditures of all state and local governments and by 1949 federal expenditures amounted to about 70% of the total with only 15% being spent at the state and local levels respectively.[14] Expressed in dollars, federal expenditures excluding debt retirement increased from $730 million in 1915 to almost $40 billion in 1949 or over 50-fold.[15] But the 1949 figures now seem relatively small, for it is estimated that during the fiscal year 1952 the federal government will spend almost $72 billion and in 1953 over $85 billion.[16] The shift in federal-state relations revealed by

[11] Senate Preparedness Subcommittee Rep. (Nov. 1951).

[12] Report on Indian Affairs, The Commission on Organization of the Executive Branch of the Government 59, 62 (March, 1949).

[13] *Information Please Almanac 1952,* 278.

[14] *Facts and Figures on Government Finance 1950-1951,* 54, Table 40 (Tax Foundation, Inc., 1950).

[15] *Id.,* 52, Table 38.

[16] Bureau of the Budget, *Budget of the U.S. for the Fiscal Year 1953,* A 5, Table 1.

these figures is further complicated by the fact that for years, both in time of war and of peace, the federal government has been spending far more than it has received with the result that the federal budget has been balanced only three of the past 21 years[17] and the federal debt has grown to towering proportions, standing today at $260 billion,[18] compared with a mere $1,263,000,000 in 1900.[19] The burden which the interest on our present national debt—not to mention its repayment—imposes on future generations is manifest; its inflationary tendencies are equally apparent. Even more ominous than the mounting national debt is the dwindling of our natural resources resulting largely from over a decade of war and preparation for war.[20]

No government, no matter how well organized, is capable of operating efficiently on such a gigantic scale,[21] and the bipartisan Hoover Commission has conclusively demonstrated that our federal government is neither well organized nor efficient. One simple illustration involving no venality will tell the whole story.

[17] 1947, 1948 and 1951.

[18] Population of the United States according to the 1950 census was 150,697,000 and the federal debt as of March 31, 1952 stood at $258,124,-000,000. 38 Fed. Res. Bull. 427 (April, 1952).

[19] Statistical Abstracts of the U.S. Dept. of Commerce (1951).

[20] See Report of the President's Materials Policy Commission (1952); Vogt, *The Road to Survival* (New York, 1948).

[21] For critiques from Democratic sources on the inefficiency of the federal administration, see Paul Douglas (U.S. Senator from Illinois), *Economy in the National Government* (Walgreen Lectures, 1951; published Chicago, 1952); Bolles, *How to Get Rich in Washington; Rich Man's Division of the Welfare State* (New York, 1952); Maass, *Muddy Waters: The Army Engineers and the Nation's Rivers* (Cambridge, Mass., 1951). Over the years the reports of the Joint Committee on Reduction of Nonessential Federal Expenditures (Senator Harry F. Byrd, Chairman) have been an invaluable source of reliable material on the inefficiency of the federal government.

Approximately one half of the 3 million purchase orders issued annually by the various federal buying agencies average less than $10 in value, yet the partial cost of processing a purchase transaction is greatly in excess of $10. In other words, the overhead cost is far more than the cost of the goods themselves.[22]

One of the most ominous developments with respect to federal spending and the encroachment of the federal government on the activities of the states is the programs of grants-in-aid carried out under the "general welfare" clause of the Constitution. Since 1934 payments by federal agencies to state and local governments have risen from $126 million to over $2¼ billion annually, an increase of over 1700%.[23] We seem to forget that the tax dollars which journey to Washington, if they ever return, come back depleted in numbers and burdened by conditions calling for the raising by state or local taxation of funds to match the grants-in-aid. Few, indeed, are the states or localities that have the wisdom and the courage to withstand being thus lured into spending for projects they cannot afford either initially to construct or later to maintain.

Not only is the executive branch of the federal government expanding enormously, but it is increasingly encroaching on fields that have always been considered the especial domain of state and local governments or of private interests. For example, the latest available figures show that in the fiscal year ended in 1951 the federal government expended over $905 million for education, not including $1.9 billion in readjustment allowances spent for

[22] Report on Supply Activities, The Commission on Organization of the Executive Branch of the Government, 27 (Feb. 1949); Task Force Report on Federal Supply System (App. B), 39 (Jan. 1949).

[23] Additional Report on Federal Grants-in-aid to States, The Joint Committee on Reduction of Nonessential Federal Expenditures, 82d Cong., 2d Sess., Sen. Doc. No. 101, Table I (1952).

veterans' education and training benefits.[24] In addition, in 1951 the President pressed Congress to initiate a program of grants-in-aid to the states for educational purposes which would require an additional $290 million for the 1953 fiscal year[25] and would grow to some $2 billion annually. The story in the field of health is equally amazing. The federal government now provides varying degrees of direct medical care to some 24 million persons[26]— one out of every six in the nation—and in 1949 some forty federal agencies spent nearly $2 billion for medical and health purposes, more than 10 times the amount spent for like purposes in 1940.[27] This outlay by the federal government represents more than one half of the moneys expended for all medical and health services in the United States[28] and is about 12 times the amount allocated for that purpose by the states themselves.[29] If this program of federal spending continues, how much longer may we expect our schools to remain under local or private control and how much longer can socialized medicine be avoided? Consider also the entry of the federal government into the field of home and in-

[24] Bureau of the Budget, *Budget of the U.S. for the Fiscal Year 1953,* 1170, Special Analysis D.

[25] *Id.*

[26] This total includes some 18,500,000 veterans eligible for certain medical benefits upon discharge; upwards of 3,000,000 members of the armed forces, their dependents, merchant seamen, and other lesser groups eligible for almost complete medical care; and over 2,000,000 federal civilian employees eligible for medical care for industrial accidents and out-patient service of the industrial type. Report on Medical Activities, The Commission on Organization of the Executive Branch of the Government, 3-4 (March, 1949).

[27] *Id.*

[28] Bureau of the Census, *Statistical Abstract of the U.S. 1951,* 225, Table 264; *Id.,* 263, Table 909.

[29] $163 million in 1950, U.S. Bureau of the Census, *Compendium of State Government Finances in 1950,* 19, Table 14 (June, 1951).

dustrial loans. As of the end of the current fiscal year it is estimated that the federal government will have issued or guaranteed home mortgage loans totaling over $28 billion;[30] that it will hold in excess of $2 billion of housing mortgages purchased from private institutions to support the mortgage market;[31] that it will have invested in public housing some $2½ billion[32] and that it will have outstanding loans to industrial and commercial concerns totaling over $608 million.[33]

When we turn in another direction—to the land—we find that the federal government is this nation's biggest landowner. Its holdings of real estate are staggering. In 1943 it owned or was in the process of acquiring 383,600,533 acres—an area equal to one fifth of the entire United States or to the combined area of 21 eastern states.[34] One might have expected the government to have reduced its land holdings following World War II, but just the opposite is true, for by 1949 it had increased its holdings by another 71,546,193 acres[35]—an area roughly one and a half times that of the State of Nebraska. Nor is the federal government's appetite for land satisfied; the battle is on between the states and the federal government with respect to the so-called "tidelands."[36]

[30] Bureau of the Budget, *Budget of the U.S. for the Fiscal Year 1953,* compiled from pp. 370 and 1176.

[31] *Id.,* 327.

[32] *Id.,* 381, 386, and 397.

[33] *Id.,* 184.

[34] Additional Report on Federal Ownership of Real Estate, The Joint Committee on Reduction of Nonessential Federal Expenditures, 78th Cong., 1st Sess., Sen. Doc. No. 130, p. 1 (1943).

[35] Committee on Public Lands, H.R. 1949, Report No. 1884.

[36] For discussions of the tidelands question see *Texas Tidelands Case, a Symposium,* 3 Baylor L. Rev. 115 (1951); Comment, *Relation of Federal and State Governments—Title of United States to Tidelands,* 50 Mich. L. Rev. 114 (1951); House Judiciary Committee, Report on H.R. 4484 (Rep. No. 695, 82d Cong., 1st Sess.) p. 47.

The stake is the ultimate control of all submerged lands—an area exceeding that of the six New England states with New York, New Jersey, Delaware and Maryland thrown in. This land orgy on the part of the federal government is by no means confined to vacant land; much productive farm land and many valuable urban properties have also been taken off the tax rolls over the years thereby reducing the revenues of the state and local governments.[37]

In much the same manner federal purchases are coming to dominate the national economy. Of our gross national product in 1929 of $103.8 billion, purchases of goods and services by state and local governments accounted for 6.9%, the federal government merely 1.3%; but of our $327.8 billion of gross national product in 1951 the state and local governments accounted for only 6%, the federal government 12.7%.[38] In other words, in the span of 22 years the direct effect of purchases by state and local governments on the gross national product fell off about 14%, while that of the federal government mounted almost 1000%.

But what should concern us most about the federal government is its phalanxed strength. The railroads, for example, are subject to the direct supervision of four federal administrative agencies—the Interstate Commerce Commission, the Railroad Retirement Board, the National Mediation Board and the Wage-Hour Division of the Labor Department—and the indirect regulation of five others—the Securities and Exchange Commission, the

[37] At the current session of Congress two bills, S. 2268 and H.R. 5223, prepared by the Bureau of the Budget and supported by the American Municipal Association have been introduced to establish the principle of federal payments in lieu of taxes to localities adversely affected by federal acquisition of property.

[38] U.S. Dept. of Commerce, Office of Economics, *National Income,* 1951 ed., pp. 17, 150; *Survey of Current Business,* p. 9 (Feb. 1952).

Internal Revenue Bureau, the Department of Defense, the Bureau of Public Roads of the Commerce Department and the General Accounting Office. Perhaps I can best make my point as to the effect of the cumulative weight of a large group of administrative agencies by telling you of an actual experience I had a number of years ago when I was appointed counsel to the receiver of a large packing concern that owed several hundred thousand dollars in processing taxes. If the Agricultural Adjustment Act[39] were valid and the taxes had to be paid, the corporation was insolvent; if the act were unconstitutional, it would be in a position to reorganize and resume business. I carefully prepared a brief on the question and was about to present the matter to the court— this was before the decision in the *Hoosac Mills* case[40]—when a lawyer from Chicago came in to see me and said he represented some packers who were interested in the question and that he had a brief he would like to show me. It was excellent. When I asked him why he did not bring a suit himself to test the constitutionality of the act, he said he represented two different packing concerns and they couldn't seem to agree as to which one should bring the suit. A day or two later in came a lawyer from Kansas City with another very good brief. He couldn't bring suit, he said, because the president of his company was in Europe and nothing could be done without his consent. A few days later in came a lawyer from Omaha, also with a fine brief. When I told him of my experience with the lawyers from Chicago and Kansas City and asked him why he didn't file a suit to test the constitutionality of the act, he asked me flatly, if I were representing a packer that had to deal with twenty different federal regulatory agencies, if I would be willing to run the risk of the wrath of each and every

[39] 48 Stat. 31 (1933), as amended 7 U.S.C. § 601 (1946).
[40] *United States v. Butler*, 297 U.S. 1 (1936).

one of them in attacking an act that was a favorite of the Administration.

Viewed from every angle, it would seem obvious that we need to reflect and then to act on the wisdom of de Tocqueville. Many of the functions now exercised by the federal government are unquestionably national in scope, but many more are not. Many of these functions can be as well or better exercised by state or local governments. The first great step in overcoming our national political imbalance is to return to the state and local governments that which is truly theirs and to free their functions from the influence of grants by the federal government. This could be done either by legislation, by judicial decision, or conceivably by constitutional revision. A federal system necessarily involves checks on the interference of the central government with the states, just as the doctrine of the separation of powers involves checks on the interference of one department in the work of the other departments of the central government. If the Congress or the courts ignore the enforcement of these checks, they do so at the peril of the welfare of the nation.

Any sketch of the growth and consequent inefficiency of the federal executive branch would be inadequate and misleading that did not make special mention of the effects of preparation for war, of waging war and of subsequent demobilization. Our concern in the matter is not historical: the mistakes in organization for World Wars I and II are being repeated in the Korean War and there is nothing to indicate that any more thought is being given to the demobilization and reconversion that we hope will some day come than there was during World War II. In none of our three recent wars was this country the aggressor. Each war was thrust upon a reluctant people, and for each of them we were unprepared. In the case of World War I there was ample excuse for this, but not so with respect to World War II or the Korean War. The organization of the executive during World War II, if indeed the word "organization" may be properly used, was fantastic. Congress in due course delegated ample power to the president, so there was no violation of the doctrine of the separation of powers.[41] The responsibility was solely the chief executive's. His efforts gave this country many more emergency agencies and a much more complicated administrative setup than in Great Britain or Canada, despite the fact that the conversion for the war effort was certainly far more thoroughgoing in Great Britain, if not in Canada. In these common-law nations with parliamentary systems the emergency agencies were organized under ministers responsible to the elected representatives of the people.[42] Here not only were most of our new establishments outside the pale of cabinet influence but many of them were expressly made responsible directly to the president, who could not possibly hope to give them any attention until a crisis made his instructions imperative. Even more important, most of the emergency agencies were created piecemeal without regard to the existence and function of the others. In studying them in chronological order it is impossible to detect any evidence of any comprehensive integrated plan for war or even for national defense. In creating emergency organizations the executive did not draw either on our experience in World War I or that of our allies in World War II. Save in special instances our administrative organization seems to have been improvised as occasion required to suit the personality of the appointing power,

[41] Principally by the First War Powers Act, 55 Stat. 838 (1941), 50 U.S.C. App. §§ 601-622 (1946).

[42] Murphy, *The British War Economy* xiv, 403 (New York, 1943); The Law Society of Upper Canada, *War Time Emergency Orders and Administrative Tribunals* 259 (Toronto, 1943).

of his appointees, and of the men they were to succeed in office or in function. It is difficult to discover reasons, other than politics or personalities, to account for many of the agencies that sprang up one after the other in rapid succession.[43]

The jurisdiction of most of the wartime agencies was so vaguely drawn as to lead inevitably to disputes as to the scope of the power conferred on them. The tendency was for each agency to drift along as best it could until disputes made necessary a direct appeal to the President. There was a marked inclination to reduce the agency heads from their rightful position as policy-makers to that of routine supervisors. In many agencies, moreover, authority was divided between an administrator and a board or advisory committe, with resultant inefficiency. Another serious defect of organization was that a wide variety of important responsibilities on advisory boards, councils and committees were thrust upon top executives who were already overloaded with their own particular duties.[44] Accordingly, they were obliged either to give only superficial attention to these added responsibilities or to neglect their primary activities. When they shared these new responsibilities jointly with other busy officials, as happened in a number of agencies, the evils of divided responsibility immediately became apparent.

Most of these difficulties might have been overcome by the preparation and execution of an over-all plan of emergency organization. Responsibility should have been carefully divided among the different agencies and adequate authority created with-

[43] For a chronological listing of the various wartime agencies, see Appendix A to the articles on *War Powers and Their Administration* in the *Annual Survey of American Law* for the years 1942 to 1946 inclusive.

[44] For a listing of the multiple officeholders and their offices, see Appendix B, *id.*

in each agency. Instead we find that agency succeeded agency with many changes in personnel especially at the executive level and with a marked tendency all along the line towards centralized personal presidential government. Each shift bespoke a failure in planning or in execution. The primary cause of many failures was the presidential unwillingness to give definite authority to the agency heads to act. All too often they were to "advise," to "recommend" or to "report," at a time when action was called for.[45] This unwillingness to delegate necessary authority was inevitably coupled with excessive centralization of authority in Washington.[46] The responsibility for this lack of organization and overcentralization of the emergency establishment rested chiefly on the President. Many of the agencies were established by executive order in the exercise of the war power. In addition Congress had vested in him an almost unlimited grant of power over both the ordinary and extraordinary establishment of the executive branch, independent commissions and government-owned corporations and the personnel of all of them. The General Accounting Office alone was withheld from his control.[47]

As the war went on, Congress exhibited apprehension at the mounting power of the executive. It made some effort to maintain control by placing a time limit on some of the powers granted to

[45] The Kilgore Committee graphically stated that they had a mere "service-station" status, Subcommittee Report No. 1, Subcommittee on War Mobilization to the Senate Committee on Military Affairs, May 13, 1943.

[46] As the Tolan Committee reporting in Oct., 1942, put it: "Many of the shortcomings of the war effort to date are traceable to the attempt to run the war from Washington." Sixth Interim Report of the Select Committee Investigating National Defense Migrations pursuant to H. Res. 113, H. Rep. No. 2589, 79th Cong., 2d Sess. (1942).

[47] See First War Powers Act, 55 Stat. 838 (1941), 50 U.S.C. App. §§ 601-622 (1946).

him.[48] Another device for restricting the President's power was to provide in legislation that Congress might terminate the power delegated to him by a concurrent resolution passed by a majority of both Houses, seeking thereby to avoid the danger of a presidential veto of any legislation curtailing his powers.[49] In a few instances periodic reports to Congress were prescribed.[50] Occasionally Congress prohibited the payment of any governmental funds to designated individuals without the prior approval of the Senate.[51] It amended the Selective Service Act to permit the President to delegate his authority thereunder but only to the director of Selective Service.[52] Numerous congressional investigating committees unearthed frequent examples of governmental inefficiency or worse and served the good purpose of preventing

[48] For example, the Emergency Price Control Act of 1942, 56 Stat. 23 (1942) § 1(b), as amended, 50 U.S.C. App. § 901 (1946); the Stabilization Act of 1942, 56 Stat. 765 (1942) §§ 6, 7(a), as amended, 50 U.S.C. App. §§ 966, 967 (1946); the Second War Powers Act, 56 Stat. 187 (1942) § 1501, as amended, 50 U.S.C. App. § 645 (1946); the Lend Lease Act, 57 Stat. 20 (1943), as amended, 22 U.S.C. § 412(c) (1946); and the Commodity Credit Corporation Act, 57 Stat. 566, 643 (1943), as amended, 15 U.S.C. § 713 (1946).

[49] For example, the First War Powers Act, 55 Stat. 841 (1941) § 401, 50 U.S.C. App. § 621 (1946); the Second War Powers Act, 56 Stat. 187 (1942) § 1501, as amended, 50 U.S.C. App. § 645 (1946); and the War Labor Disputes Act, 57 Stat. 163, 168 (1943), 50 U.S.C. App. §§ 1501, 1510 (1946). Whether this device would avail in the event of a contest was not without question. See White, *The Concurrent Resolution in Congress,* 35 Am. Pol. Sci. Rev. 886 (1941).

[50] For example, the Lend-Lease Act, 55 Stat. 32 (1941) § 5(b), 22 U.S.C. § 414 (1946).

[51] The Urgent Deficiency Appropriation Act of 1943 prohibited payment of any governmental funds to Goodwin B. Watson, William E. Dodd, Jr., and Robert M. Lovett, appointees of the President, without prior approval of the Senate. 57 Stat. 431 (1943) § 304.

[52] 57 Stat. 598 (1943), 50 U.S.C. App. § 310 (1946).

the recurrence of such mistakes.[53] But in general effective congressional control of the wartime establishment was conspicuous by its absence. Congress had become so inured over the preceding quarter century to the practice of delegating legislative and judicial powers to independent agencies and to the established departments of the executive branch of the government without retaining any effective control thereof that it found it difficult in wartime to set up effective controls over the grant of vast emergency powers.

One concrete example will serve to illustrate the wartime confusion. The Office of Dependency Benefits was created by an act of Congress in 1942.[54] In the course of the five years of its existence the Army branch drew some 244 million checks aggregating over $14 billion. This office was not mentioned in the successive issues of the United States Government Manual or of the Congressional Directory until late in 1945, despite the fact that the omission had several times been pointed out and notwithstanding that the Army branch regularly filed excellent annual reports on its activities. Curiously enough the Navy branch of the Office of Dependency Benefits never printed any reports. A request I addressed to the Secretary of the Navy and which was forwarded to the Navy branch at Cleveland inquiring as to the number of dependency checks and the total amount thereof issued by it went unanswered for several weeks. Finally it elicited a telegram stating that the "request is of unusual nature and compilation of data requested will involve considerable employee time and expense" and requesting me to "indicate purpose for which report requested

---

[53] See sections on "Congressional Investigating Committees," *War Powers and Their Administration*, 1943 *Annual Survey of American Law* 139-154; 1944 *id.*, 240-259; 1945 *id.*, 303-321; 1946 *id.*, 280-286.

[54] 56 Stat. 381 (1942), as amended, 37 U.S.C. § 201 (1946).

will be used and your interest therein." Truly a government that nobody knows and a government that at times does not seem to wish to be known!

Reconversion to peace proved even more difficult and haphazard than the building up of the emergency establishment, and necessarily so for the task of applying the brakes to the military machine was complicated by the necessity of simultaneously building up and putting into operation the peacetime economy of the country. As wartime instrumentalities disappeared reconversion agencies sprang up in their place.[55] But in both the old and the new emergency agencies the dubious practice of multiple office-holding at the policy level continued unabated and it was not until 1947 that most vexatious controls disappeared.[56] The two encouraging aspects of the reconversion period were, first, the reports of the numerous congressional investigating committees whose work had to be taken seriously because they were manned primarily by committeemen of the same political party as the President, and, second, the resumption by Congress of its responsibility for the organization of the executive branch of government which was reflected in such legislation as the Reorganization Act of 1945,[57] the Government Corporation Control Act (1945),[58] and the National Security Act of 1947[59] creating a single department of national defense.

Is it not obvious that no more important task confronts the chief executive and the Congress than that of availing themselves of the best management minds in the country to plan the greatest

[55] See "The Reconversion Period," *War Powers and Their Administration,* 1946 *Annual Survey of American Law* 259-305.

[56] See "The Movement Toward Reconversion" in 1947 *id.,* 264.

[57] 59 Stat. 613 (1945), 5 U.S.C. § 133(y) (1946).

[58] 59 Stat. 597 (1945), 31 U.S.C. § 841 (1946).

[59] 61 Stat. 495 (1947), as amended, 5 U.S.C. § 401 *et seq.* (Supp. 1951).

rearmament and industrial mobilization in our history and the reconversion and demobilization that will one day supersede the present emergency? And are not these problems the special concern of lawyers as the traditional exponents of individual freedom?

It was the breakdown of the administrative organization in World War II that ultimately induced Congress to pass the Lodge-Brown Act of 1947,[60] calling for a survey to induce "economy, efficiency and improved service in the transaction of public business." The necessity of a reorganization of the executive branch of the government had been called to the attention of Congress by several presidents, but never in more emphatic language than that used by President Roosevelt in transmitting to Congress the report, hereinbefore mentioned, of his Committee on Administrative Management:

> The executive structure of the Government is sadly out of date. I am not the first President to report to the Congress that antiquated machinery stands in the way of effective administration and of adequate control by the Congress. Theodore Roosevelt, William H. Taft, Woodrow Wilson, and Herbert Hoover made repeated but not wholly successful efforts to deal with the problem.....

> In these troubled years of world history a self-government cannot long survive unless that government is an effective and efficient agency to serve mankind and carry out the will of the Nation....

> Neither the President nor the Congress can exercise effective supervision and direction over such a chaos of establishments, nor can overlapping, duplication, and contradictory policies be avoided.

[60] 61 Stat. 499 (1947), as amended, 5 U.S.C. App. § 171 (Supp. 1951).

The Committee has not spared me; they say, what has been common knowledge for 20 years, that the President cannot adequately handle his responsibilities; that he is overworked; that it is humanly impossible, under the system which we have, for him fully to carry out his constitutional duty as Chief Executive, because he is overwhelmed with minor details and needless contacts arising directly from the bad organization and equipment of the Government. I can testify to this. With my predecessors who have said the same thing over and over again, I plead guilty.[61]

Pursuant to the Lodge-Brown Act President Truman appointed a distinguished bipartisan Commission of twelve with former President Herbert Hoover as chairman,[62] and the Commission in turn was aided by 24 task forces composed of 300 outstanding citizens drawn from various walks of life. These task forces, assisted by full-time research staffs of the ablest specialists and consultants in the country, investigated every agency in the executive arm of government with the view to ascertaining the facts and making recommendations for modernizing the governmental processes. After two years of intensive work the Commission and the task forces filed their reports.[63] It is claimed that the

[61] Message to the Congress, Jan. 12, 1937 (reprinted, pp. iii-v of the Committee's Report).

[62] The Commission on Organization of the Executive Branch of the Government is commonly referred to as the Hoover Commission. Other members of the Commission were Secretary of State Dean Acheson, vice-chairman; former Civil Service Commissioner Arthur S. Fleming; Secretary of Defense James V. Forrestal; Senator George D. Aiken of Vermont; former Ambassador to Great Britain Joseph P. Kennedy; Senator John L. McClellan of Arkansas; Michigan professor of political science James K. Pollock; Representative Clarence J. Brown of Ohio; Representative Carter Wanasco of Alabama; and former Assistant to the President James H. Rowe, Jr.

[63] Nineteen reports were filed in all, the final report being submitted to the Congress on May 20, 1949.

acceptance of the recommendations of these reports will effect an annual saving of from $3 billion to $5 billion.[64] The Commission was not charged with the responsibility for examining into the question of whether any particular governmental service was essential, although much might have been said on that subject, but it was merely charged with the responsibility for recommending steps for improving the efficiency and economy in 'the functions of government they found in existence.[65]

To strengthen the executive branch of the government and to restore efficiency to its operation, the Hoover Commission made numerous specific recommendations, centering around four principles each requiring Congressional endorsement: first, the granting of permanent powers for reorganization to the President; second, the removal of all restrictions on the organization of the office of the President; third, the enlarging of the authority of department and agency heads so as to permit them to select their subordinates and assign departmental functions to them and to allocate funds within their departments; and fourth, to inaugurate a broad program of reform aimed at improved management in the fields of personnel, budgets, accounting and general administrative services and to regroup governmental functions by major purpose. If these recommendations were to be followed the number of agencies reporting directly to the President would be reduced from 52 to 30 and the various activities of the federal

[64] Congressional Record, p. 7597 (June 18, 1952).

[65] "As a matter of principle the Commission has not been concerned with matters of substantive policy. In practice, however, it has often been extremely difficult to separate policy from administration, although a conscientious effort has been made to do so. The Commission focused its attention mainly on how efficiently present services were being performed, rather than on the question of whether they should or should not be performed." Concluding Report, 2-3 (May, 1949).

government, in order to eliminate waste, duplication and confusion, would be organized in six comprehensive programs: (1) natural resources, (2) commerce and industry, (3) social welfare, (4) business enterprises, (5) foreign affairs, and (6) national defense. Lack of time precludes a further enumeration here of the specific recommendations put forward to accomplish these reforms, but it is to be noted that the National Citizens Committee for the Hoover Report under the chairmanship of President Robert L. Johnson of Temple University, has just announced that only 52% of the recommendations of the Commission have been adopted by Congress or the executive branch. Many of the basic recommendations which would effect the greatest economies still remain to be accepted.

Significant though the work of the Hoover Commission is, we must constantly keep in mind the fact previously mentioned, that it did not consider whether the functions of government it was studying were essential or, if essential, whether they should be retained in the federal government or turned over to state and local governments. Without such a study and action thereon the present imbalance of the federal executive department in the national economy will continue and become even more aggravated. But there is another study that is equally important. What was needed after World War I and again after World War II and what will be needed after the present drive for rearmament is over is a special committee of the Congress charged with the duty of seeing to it that the individual freedom that is inevitably restricted in time of emergency is returned to the citizens uncurtailed after the emergency is over. The matter should also be a subject for the special attention of the bar, of our institutions of learning, and of the people generally.

The congested imbalance of the executive branch of the federal government at Washington that we have been describing in peace and in war, in preparation for war and in recovery from war, and the limitations on the freedom of the individual that have been imposed in the several phases of the war cycle constitute the background against which we must study the present-day applications of the doctrine of the separation of powers in the executive branch of the federal government.[66]

When we turn to the legislative aspects of the work of the executive branch of the federal government we cannot fail to be impressed with its vast range. For example, the President's power to issue the customary Thanksgiving proclamation rests on no congressional grant of authority, but in 1939 when the President, to aid the Christmas trade, saw fit to advance Thanksgiving from the last to the next to the last Thursday in November, he upset, among others, calendar and diary manufacturers. Their protests would probably have gone unheeded had not the change also interfered with that major American industry known as football. It is a far cry from such simple lawmaking proclamations to the vast powers which the President exercises in foreign affairs both in wartime and in peace, either alone or with Senate or Congressional approval. One has only to utter such words as "secret agreements" or "undeclared war" to sense the seriousness to the nation of the exercise of the none-too-well-defined powers of presidential law-making under the Constitution in the field of foreign affairs. With our present position in world affairs these problems are likely to grow more acute both in peace and in war, a situation which has led to serious discussion of the necessity of amending

[66] For widely divergent viewpoints on the doctrine of the separation of powers today, see Kinnane, *Some Observations on Separation of Powers,* 38 A.B.A.J. 19 (1952); Coil, *Remarks on the Separation of Powers: A Reply to Professor Kinnane,* 38 A.B.A.J. 365 (1952).

the Constitution with respect to treaty-making and executive agreements.[67]

In the ordinary processes of legislation, moreover, the last quarter of a century has witnessed a tremendous rise of presidential power in initiating legislation, in expediting its progress through the Congress and in vetoing undesired legislation. Dr. Ernest S. Griffith, Director of the Legislative Reference Service of the Library of Congress, estimates that fully 80 per cent of the important legislation of the first three years of the administration of President Franklin D. Roosevelt originated in the White House or in the executive departments.[68] The habit then formed has not

[67] See Senate Joint Resolution 130 introduced by Senator Bricker on Feb. 7, 1952, proposing an amendment to the Constitution relative to the making of treaties and executive agreements, and Senate Joint Resolution 122 introduced by Senator McCarran on Jan. 21, 1952, proposing congressional limitations on executive agreements. These two resolutions have touched off renewed debate on the subject. On Feb. 26, 1952, the House of Delegates of the American Bar Association, rejecting the recommendation of its Section of International and Comparative Law to delay action on the subject, adopted a resolution proposed by its Committee on Peace and Law calling for an amendment to the Constitution as follows: "A provision of a treaty which conflicts with any provision of this Constitution shall not be of any force or effect. A treaty shall become effective as internal law in the United States only through legislation by Congress which it could enact under its delegated powers in the absence of such treaty." 38 A.B.A.J. 435-436 (1952). Subsequent to the delivery of this lecture the Association of the Bar of the City of New York went on record as opposing any such amendment, Report on S. J. Res. 130 of its Committees on Federal Legislation and on International Law (Apr. 28, 1952). See also Holman, *Treaty Law—A Threat to American Rights,* 20 J.B.A. Kan. 253 (1952); Sutherland, *Restricting the Treaty Power,* 65 Harv. L. Rev. 1305 (1952); Finch, *Treaty-Clause Amendment: The Case for the Association,* 38 A.B.A.J. 467 (1952); Chafee, *The Constitutional Amendment of the Treaty Making Power,* 75 N.J.L.J. 233, 241 (1952).

[68] Griffith, *Congress: Its Contemporary Role* 65 (New York, 1951).

disappeared, especially in fiscal and economic matters. In these fields the President has the great advantage of the technical skill and continuous services of the Bureau of the Budget and of the Council of Economic Advisers, which the Congress is not equipped to match though legislation in these fields is peculiarly its responsibility. In effect the President has acquired the powers of the English prime minister over the introduction of legislation without the correlative duties to the legislative branch imposed on the prime minister under the English practice. In expediting legislation through Congress the President has not only the prestige of party leadership, but also the power of patronage resulting from his right to appoint a multitude of officials. Equally important is the presidential veto power, for as Dr. Griffith says: "Only under exceptional circumstances is the veto overridden. One reason is that certain members vote for a particular measure, knowing it will be vetoed." [69] All of these legislative powers of the President are within the Constitution, but over the last quarter of a century they have served to exalt the place of the chief executive in the legislative process at the expense of the Congress.[70]

When we consider the aggregate amount of executive legislation, however, we are quickly impressed with the fact that the executive branch of the government, including here the administrative agencies, derives more power by delegation from Congress than it does from the Constitution itself. Delegated legislative power, despite the maxim "*Delegatus non potest delegari*," is nothing new in our law. Delegation of legislative power to the political subdivisions of the states has long been deemed fundamental to

[69] *Op. cit.*, 27.

[70] See Corwin, *The President, Office and Powers, 1787-1948* (3d ed., rev., New York, 1948); Hart, *The American Presidency in Action*, 1789 (New York, 1948).

the American constitutional system. The delegation of legislative power to the federal executive has come more slowly and out of necessity. At first it was confined to permitting the President to pass on simple facts requiring no discretion,[71] then on more complicated facts requiring the exercise of discretion,[72] and then on still more complicated facts that he could arrive at only with expert administrative assistance.[73] The trend was irresistible. The greatest growth, however, in the delegation of legislative power by Congress is to be traced to the organization of the Interstate Commerce Commission in 1887[74] with its commingled legislative, investigatory, prosecuting and adjudicating functions. The Commission set the administrative pattern which has been so generally employed in both state and national governments. As a result, to quote Elihu Root, speaking in 1916, "The old doctrine prohibiting the delegation of legislative power has virtually retired from the field and given up the fight." [75] Yet illustrating the danger of prophecy, when the Congress undertook in the National Industrial Recovery Act of 1933[76] to give the President power to approve "codes of fair competition" for various industries, the Supreme Court disapproved the virtually unfettered nature of the grant and termed it "delegation running riot." [77] Standards of delegation must be set up, and while they may be vague, they

[71] *The Brig Aurora v. United States,* 11 U.S. 382 (1813).

[72] *Field v. Clark,* 143 U.S. 649 (1892).

[73] *J. W. Hampton Jr., & Co. v. United States,* 276 U.S. 394 (1928).

[74] Interstate Commerce Act, 24 Stat. 383 (1887), as amended, 49 U.S.C. § 11 (1946).

[75] *Addresses on Government and Citizenship* 534 (col. and ed. by Bacon and Scott, Cambridge, Mass., 1916).

[76] 48 Stat. 195 (1933).

[77] Concurring opinion of Mr. Justice Cardozo in *Schechter v. United States,* 205 U.S. 495, at 553 (1935). See also *Panama Refining Co. v. Ryan,* 293 U.S. 388 (1935).

cannot be so vague as not to furnish any guide to the administrator or the court, nor, it seems, must they cover too much ground. The alternative to the fixing of adequate standards is government by personal edict with its attendant uncertainties and excesses.[78]

Probably the widest delegation of legislative power that has thus far been sustained by the courts even as an emergency measure was that granted to the Office of Price Administration in World War II.[79] It was authorized to control prices by regulations rather than by adjudication before the agency. There had

[78] There are in the federal government, however, those to whom uncertainty has its appeal. Speaking before a convention of the American Federation of Labor at San Francisco on Sept. 18, 1951, Secretary of Labor Tobin said in discussing the subject of labor relations: "The kind of law I have in mind would make government intervention unattractive by preserving the element of uncertainty and the element of flexibility. Neither side would know when the government would intervene or if the government would intervene. The President might appoint a fact-finding board or a mediator. He might appoint them with or without the power to make recommendations. He might require the workers to stay on the job while the board deliberated or he might leave them free to strike.

"And the President might not appoint any fact-finders at all. He might seize with or without fact-finding. And if he seized he might have the government operate it for the account of the government. The notion that seizure should be handled in such a way that the employer goes on collecting his profits and only the union is hurt has no place in a fair and equitable labor law. The parties must not only be kept from knowing whether the President will seize, they must not know what form the seizure will take." Proceedings of the 70th Annual Convention at p. 256.

[79] Originally created by Executive Order 8734, on April 11, 1941, principally to prepare plans and legislation for actual price control. There followed the Emergency Price Control Act of 1942, 56 Stat. 23, as amended, 50 U.S.C. App. § 901 *et seq.*, (1946), which created the office as an independent agency and granted the Price Administrator price and rent-fixing authority. The constitutionality of the act was upheld in *Lockerty v. Phillips,* 319 U.S. 182 (1943); *Yakus v. United States,* 321 U.S. 414 (1944); and *Bowles v. Willingham,* 321 U.S. 503 (1944).

been other agencies that had proceeded by rule-making such as
the Bituminous Coal Commission[80] but there the right to judicial
review was never questioned. Here the purpose of the draftsmen
of the legislation, a congressional investigating committee reported, was to place final and nonreviewable authority in the hands
of the director.[81] Throughout the Emergency Price Control Act
there is a studied effort to comply with the constitutional forms
while withholding their substance. On the one hand the agency
enforced its regulations by injunction proceedings[82] or by criminal
proceedings in the courts.[83] On the other hand, the act precluded
the individual affected from resorting either to the regular federal
or state courts to question the validity of any of the regulations
issued by the agency, review being available only in a special
Emergency Court of Appeals,[84] to which he could only go after
he had exhausted his administrative remedies within the agency.[85]
In providing rule-making procedures the statute adopted numer-

[80] The Bituminous Coal Conservation Act of 1935, 49 Stat. 991, originally created the Commission but was declared unconstitutional in *Carter
v. Carter Coal Co.,* 298 U.S. 328 (1936). Thereafter the Commission was
recreated by the Bituminous Coal Act of 1937, 50 Stat. 72, 15 U.S.C.A.
§ 828 (1940). Effective July 1, 1939, its functions were transferred to the
Bituminous Coal Division of the Department of the Interior by the President's Reorganization Plan No. 2 approved by Congress on June 7, 1939.
The 1937 Act was upheld in *Sunshine Anthracite Coal Co. v. Adkins,*
310 U.S. 381 (1940).

[81] Second Intermediate Report of the Select Committee to Investigate
Executive Agencies, pursuant to H. Res. 102, H. Rep. No. 862, 78th Cong.,
1st Sess. 3-4 (1943).

[82] § 205(a).

[83] § 205(b).

[84] § 204.

[85] *Safeway Stores, Inc. v. Brown,* 138 F. 2d 278 (Emerg. Ct. of App.
1943); cert. denied *sub. nom. Safeway Stores, Inc. v. Bowles,* 320 U.S. 797
(1943).

ous devices designed to block any contest of the price regulations issued. The administrator was not required to make findings.[86] He was not required to hold hearings though he was obliged to advise and consult with representative members of the industry of his own choosing "so far as practicable" *after* the issuance of regulations "at the request of a substantial portion of the industry." [87] Even these illusory limitations on the making of price regulations could be avoided by the issuance of temporary price regulations.[88] An aggrieved party might protest against a regulation by "affidavits or other written evidence" and he might file a brief, but there was no hearing provided for.[89] The administrator was authorized to take "official notice of economic data and other facts." [90] What this economic data and other facts were, the aggrieved party never knew, nor was he permitted to present testimony or cross-examine a witness against him.[91] The record on appeal to the Emergency Court of Appeals was to contain "such portions of the proceeding in connection with the protest as are material under the complaint" and "so far as practicable" the economic data and other facts of which the administrator had taken official notice.[92] The Emergency Court of Appeals was specifically prohibited from issuing "any temporary restraining order or interlocutory decree staying or restraining, in whole or in part, the effectiveness of any regulation.[93] Even if, after hear-

---

[86] § 2(a).

[87] *Id.*

[88] *Id.*

[89] § 203(a).

[90] § 203(b).

[91] § 203(c). This section was amended on June 30, 1944, to provide for a hearing before a board of review within the Office of Price Administration itself in the event a protest was denied. 56 Stat. 638.

[92] § 204(a).

[93] § 204(c).

ing, it held such a regulation unlawful, the "effectiveness of a judgment . . . shall be postponed until the expiration of thirty days." [94] If the administrator applied to the Supreme Court for a writ of certiorari, then the judgment was further postponed until final action by the Supreme Court.[95]

The Emergency Price Control Act resulted in what may well be the most dangerous decisions, insofar as the existence of the doctrine of the separation of powers is concerned, that were ever handed down by the Supreme Court.[96] Thus in *Yakus v. United States*[97] it was held that no court except the Emergency Court of Appeals and, on appeal, the Supreme Court had jurisdiction or power to consider the validity of a price regulation and that therefore a defendant was precluded from setting up the invalidity of such a regulation as a defense to a criminal prosecution under the act. This judicial approval of a legislative device to strip the courts of their power constitutes a continuing threat to the integrity, independence and equality of the judicial branch of the government. The effect of limiting the exercise of judicial power, once conferred, was well summarized by Mr. Justice Rutledge in a dissent in which Mr. Justice Murphy joined:

> It is one thing for Congress to withhold jurisdiction. It is an entirely another to confer it and direct that it be exercised in a manner inconsistent with constitutional requirements or, what in some instances may be the same thing, without regard to them. Once it is held that Congress can require the courts criminally to enforce unconstitutional laws or statutes, including regulations, or to do so without regard to their validity,

[94] § 204(b).
[95] § 204(d).
[96] *Lockerty v. Phillips,* 319 U.S. 182 (1943); *Yakus v. United States,* 321 U.S. 414 (1944); *Bowles v. Willingham,* 321 U.S. 503 (1944).
[97] 321 U.S. 414 (1944).

the way will have been found to circumvent the supreme law and, what is more, to make the courts parties to doing so. This Congress cannot do. . . . Whenever the judicial power is called into play, it is responsible directly to the fundamental law and no other authority can intervene to force or authorize the judicial body to disregard it. The problem therefore is not solely one of individual right or due process of law. It is equally one of the separation and independence of the powers of government and of the constitutional intergrity of the judicial process, more especially in criminal trials.[98]

One cannot read the act and the decisions upholding it without being reminded of a line in a statement of Miss Ellen Wilkinson, M. P., concurred in by Harold J. Laski and appended to the report of the English Committee on Ministers' Powers: "Nothing is so dangerous in a democracy as a safeguard which appears to be adequate but which is really a facade." [99]

What safeguards are there from executive legislation? Congress could equip itself with budgetary and economic staffs at least as efficient as those of the executive, and it surely has no geater duty. It could grant powers to the executive or an administrative agency on a temporary, trial basis and it could repeal old grants of authority when they were found to be unnecessary or unworkable. It could insist that all rules and regulations be laid before it in one form or another before they become effective, as in England where they receive the attention of the Scrutiny Committee aided by the counsel to the Speaker;[100] or it might require as in Connecticut that all regulations be examined by the attorney general

[98] 321 U.S. at 468.

[99] Annex VI, p. 138 of the report presented by the Lord High Chancellor to Parliament, April, 1932 (published in London by H. M. Stationery Office, 1936).

[100] Schwartz, *Law and the Executive in Britain* 116 *et seq.* (New York, 1949).

and submitted to the next session of the legislature for review with public hearings before the appropriate committees.[101] Congress, of course, may conduct investigations, but investigations generally are undertaken and corrective legislation enacted only after a situation has become acute. But whatever the means, it is essential for the maintenance of a proper balance between the executive and the legislative branches of the federal government that Congress take positive action to strengthen itself against encroachments by the President.[102]

While the procedure of the executive departments and of the administrative agencies in promulgating delegated legislation has not caused as much general controversy as the administrative processes of adjudication, it is of equal practical importance, as experience with the Office of Price Administration and other wartime agencies has demonstrated. Before the report and studies of the Attorney General's Committee on Administrative Procedure were published in 1941,[103] the matter of administrative law-making was almost *terra incognita*. The majority and the minority of the Attorney General's Committee differed on three basic

[101] Conn. Gen. Stat. (1949 Rev.) §§ 280-287. See also *Congressional Oversight of Administrative Agencies,* a report of the Committee on Administrative Law of the Association of the Bar of the City of New York, 5 The Record 11 (Jan. 1950).

[102] For a proposal that the president construct his cabinet from a joint legislative council created by both Houses of Congress, see Corwin, *The President, Office and Powers, 1787-1948,* 353-364 (3d ed. rev., New York, 1948). See also Cheever and Haviland, *American Foreign Policy and the Separation of Powers* 175 (Cambridge, Mass. 1952).

[103] The Report of the Committee, appointed by the Attorney General in 1939 at the suggestion of the President, was submitted on Jan. 22, 1941, and transmitted by the Attorney General to Congress on Jan. 24, 1941. (U.S. Gov't Printing Office, Washington, D.C., 1941).

propositions, the first of which was the desirability of a legislative statement of standards of fair procedure, the minority favoring it, the majority opposing.[104] After five years of investigation, analysis and debate the federal Administrative Procedure Act was unanimously passed by both Houses of Congress in 1946.[105] It is designed to protect the individual citizen from the hazards of uncertain and slipshod administrative procedures resulting in unfair and arbitrary action, while at the same time seeking to preserve the flexibility, the resourcefulness and progressiveness of the administrative agency at its best. It sets up standards of administrative procedure conforming to a considerable degree to the suggestion of the minority of the Attorney General's Committee on Administrative Procedure.[106] The Act is comprehensive in scope and in terms applies to the executive and all administrative agencies, but exceptions are provided for as to certain types of functions. Thus, for example, while there is no exemption under the Act for the War and Navy Departments as such, Section 2(a) exempts courts-martial, military commissions, and military or naval authority exercised in the field in time of war or in occupied territory. Another typical exception is found in Section 3 relating to Public Information, which is applicable, "Except to the extent that there is involved (1) any function of the United States requiring secrecy in the public interest or (2) any matter relating solely to the internal management of any agency . . ." Unfortunately since the passage of the Act about a score of exceptions

[104] See "Statements of Additional Views and Recommendations" of Messrs. McFarland, Stason, and Vanderbilt, *id.,* at p. 203.

[105] 60 Stat. 237 (1946), 5 U.S.C. § 1001 *et seq.* (1946).

[106] See Report, *op. cit.,* "Appendix to Statement of Additional Views and Recommendations," p. 217.

have been written into it, but a bill to remove most of these added exceptions has passed the Senate and is now before the House.[107]

The Act marks the beginning of a new era in American administrative law in that Congress has at last recognized the importance, even though inadequately, of administrative procedures. While like all legislation it involves compromises, for the first time it set forth the procedural principles on which Congress expects the administrative agencies to operate. It proceeds on the premise that the executive as well as the citizen should be subject to law. The specific reasons for insisting on a legislative statement of standards of fair procedure were thus stated in the minority report of the Attorney General's Committee:

> Administrative agencies are peculiarly sensitive to procedural and substantive provisions of statute, however general their terms—far more than to the statements of courts. Where controversy is stirred over a specific agency, we have only to look to the legislation under which it acts. If Congress has given constant attention, as it has to the Interstate Commerce Commission, a better result has been achieved. Without impairing government, a legislative statement of principles will go far toward dispelling the cloud that hovers over the administrative process. It will guide administrators and protect the citizen far more than the judicial review of particular administrative cases, which is available only to those few who can afford it. What is needed is not a detailed code but a set of principles and a settlement of legislative policy. The prescribed pattern need not be, and should not be, a rigid mold. There should be ample room for necessary changes and full allowance for differing needs of different agencies.
>
> Such a statement would be of invaluable assistance to the private persons on whom powers of government impinge, for they

[107] S. 1770 introduced by Senator McCarran passed the Senate Oct. 11, 1951.

could learn more readily and clearly when, where, and how to proceed. Greater cooperation with Government officials would be assured. It would be of inestimable value to government itself by helping to alleviate the disrespect, distrust, and fear now felt by too large a percentage of citizens. Finally, there is reason to believe that administrative officials would welcome the assistance of general procedural instructions which, instead of leaving them groping in the dark, would furnish a pattern of action. . . .

One further purpose must be served by any such legislative statement. In several respects most agencies lack one or more essential powers of administration. A galaxy of regulatory statutes, for example, speaks solely in terms of the Secretary of Agriculture, thus ignoring the essential need for the Secretary to utilize assistance. Again, agencies are without formal direction or authority to issue types of rules or regulations which are indispensable if the citizen is to be informed of the organization and policy of any agency. Congress should recognize, specify, and confer these and other necessary powers. Otherwise, administration is unduly complicated; necessity leads to subterfuge, inactivity, hardship to the citizen, or the public, and unwarranted expense to the Government; and the cry for justice is thwarted by lack of the simple means to do justice.[108]

Section 4 of the Act gives new significance to administrative rule-making, both from the standpoint of the administrative agency and of the individual citizen by providing that due notice of proposed rule-making shall be published in the Federal Register, except where actual notice is given or where the agency for good cause finds—and incorporates the findings in the rules issued—that notice is "impracticable, unnecessary or contrary to the public interest." [109]

[108] *Op. cit.,* 215-216.
[109] § 4(a).

Rule-making may be either informal or formal depending on the requirements in the statute creating the agency in question.[110] Formal rule-making requires a hearing so as to make a record.[111] Where the statute creating the agency requires such a hearing, any aggrieved party is given precisely the same rights in respect to a hearing and the decisions that would follow the hearing as would any litigant in a contested case before the agency. Unfortunately the Congress has thus far required a record in rule-making in very few instances, though the procedure has been used in such important statutes as the Food, Drug and Cosmetic Act[112] and the Fair Labor Standards Act.[113] The pattern stands, however, for a procedure that Congress should investigate further. On informal rule-making, after notice has been given, interested persons are given an opportunity to submit their data in writing and to present their arguments either in writing or orally as the agency may elect. After a consideration of all of the relevant data submitted the agency incorporates in the rules it adopts a "concise general statement of their basis and purposes." [114] While informal rule-making falls far short of the safeguards afforded by formal rule-making, it nevertheless affords the citizen greater rights than he has in dealing with the Congress or state legislatures.

In the field of administrative jurisdiction the greatest controversy has been over the commingling of investigating, prosecuting and judicial functions in one man or one body of men. President Roosevelt's Committee on Administrative Management was strongly opposed to the practice:

[110] § 4(b).
[111] §§ 4(b), 7, 8.
[112] 52 Stat. 1040 (1938), 21 U.S.C. § 321 (1946).
[113] 52 Stat. 1060 (1938), 29 U.S.C. § 201 (1946).
[114] § 4(b).

At the same time [as it executes its other duties] the independent commission is obliged to carry on judicial functions under conditions which threaten the impartial performance of that judicial work. The discretionary work of the administrator is merged with that of the judge. Pressures and influences properly enough directed toward officers responsible for formulating and administering policy constitute an unwholesome atmosphere in which to adjudicate private rights. But the mixed duties of the commissions render escape from their subversive influences impossible.

Furthermore, the same men are obliged to serve both as prosecutors and as judges. This not only undermines judicial fairness; it weakens public confidence in that fairness. Commission decisions affecting private rights and conduct are under the suspicion of being rationalizations of the preliminary findings which the commission, in the role of prosecutor, presented to itself.

The independent commission, in short, provides the proper working conditions neither for administration nor adjudication. It fails to provide responsibility for the first; it does not provide complete independence for the second.[115]

The minority of the Attorney General's Committee was likewise opposed,[116] citing the traditional division between prosecutor and trial court in ordinary criminal litigation and the Bureau of Internal Revenue and the Board of Tax Appeals, now the Tax Court, as outstanding examples of a successful division of functions between rule-maker and prosecutor on the one hand and judge on the other. Another more recent but equally important example of complete separation of functions is to be found in the work

---

[115] Report on Administrative Management in the Government of the United States, Jan. 1937, at p. 40 (U.S. Gov't Printing Office, Washington, D.C. 1937).

[116] *Op. cit.,* 203-209.

of the National Labor Relations Board under the Taft-Hartley Act.[117]

It may be necessary for an agency in its infancy to exercise all three powers in exploring the field of its activities, but as it reaches maturity its functions should be separated so as to eliminate the dangers inherent in omnipotency. But the administrative agencies with commingled prosecuting and adjudicatory powers had seemingly become a tradition too strong for Congress to overcome in most instances. Congress in the Administrative Procedure Act decided against complete separation, but it did make an effort to provide some safeguards within the existing framework of the agency by internal separation. There must be notice given of hearings and of the issues involved[118] and an opportunity to present facts, arguments and offers of settlement.[119] The hearing officer shall be independent of any officers engaged in investigative or prosecuting functions of the agency and shall not "consult any person or party on any fact in issue unless upon notice and opportunity for all parties to participate," [120] and shall make the initial decision or a recommended decision.[121] The power to make the initial decision is admirable, but the limitation of the hearing officer's power merely to recommending a decision for agency approval leaves much to be desired. Persons required to appear before an agency shall be entitled to have counsel [122] and agency

---

[117] National Labor Relations Act as amended by Labor Management Relations Act of 1947 (Taft-Hartley) §§ 6, 9, 10; 29 U.S.C. §§ 156, 159, (c) (d), 160 (Supp. 1949).

[118] § 5(a).

[119] § 5(b).

[120] § 5(c).

[121] § 7(b).

[122] § 6(a).

subpoenas [123] and they shall be entitled to get copies of records.[124] No order shall be made "except upon consideration of the whole record . . . as supported by and in accordance with the reliable, probative and substantial evidence" [125]—a very real advance if properly construed by the courts. Either prior to or after a decision by a hearing officer the parties shall be given an opportunity to submit findings, exceptions and supporting reasons, and the record shall show the ruling on each.[126] Though the Act is a long step forward, the internal separation of prosecuting and adjudicatory functions in an agency inevitably falls short of giving the individual the protection to which he has been traditionally entitled in all justiciable controversies. One wonders, indeed, if the individual can ever be given adequate protection, human nature being what it is, when the prosecuting and adjudicatory functions are still subject to the control of the same agency heads.

The final question on which the members of the Attorney General's Committee split was on the related issue of the scope of judicial review. The minority urged that until complete external separation of functions was provided, judicial review must be given a wide scope,[127] but this view was not taken by the Congress. Section 10 of the Act provides that persons adversely affected or aggrieved by any agency action shall be entitled to judicial review[128] in statutory form, or in the absence or inadequacy thereof, by any applicable form of legal action.[129] Every agency action made reviewable by statute and every final agency

[123] § 6(c).
[124] § 7(d).
[125] § 7(c).
[126] § 8(b).
[127] *Op. cit.,* 209-212.
[128] § 10(a).
[129] § 10(b).

action for which there is no adequate remedy in any court shall be subject to judicial review.[130] Agencies or reviewing courts may issue stays.[131] So far as necessary to decision, the reviewing courts shall decide all relevant questions of law and shall compel agency action unlawfully withheld or unreasonably delayed, and shall set aside agency action found arbitrary or capricious, not in accordance with law or unsupported by substantial evidence.[132] The deficiencies of judicial review I shall discuss at length in my last lecture. Some of the defects of limited judicial review might have been overcome if the Civil Service Commission had acted to create a strong corps of examiners. This Act provides that the hearing officers, called examiners, are subject to civil service, are to be assigned cases in rotation, and are removable "only for good cause established and determined by the Civil Service Commission" after hearing.[133]

Seams have appeared and, as in the case of the Federal Rules of Civil Procedure after a similar trial period, it may sooner or later require a revision, but even with its defects it has gone far to achieve the goal asserted by Mr. Justice Brandeis, "In the development of our liberty, insistence upon procedural regularity has been a large factor." [134]

With respect to the organization and operation of the executive branch, the Congress has it entirely within its power through the acceptance of the recommendations of the Hoover Commission to cut substantially government expenses and to increase efficiency. By strengthening the federal Administrative Procedure Act it

[130] § 10(c).
[131] § 10(d).
[132] § 10(e).
[133] § 11.
[134] Dissenting opinion in *Burdeau v. McDowell,* 256 U.S. 465, at 477 (1921).

can assure to the citizen the rule of law in administrative rule-making and adjudication. Congress may also ameliorate the trend toward centralization due to the excessive vesting of power in the executive arm of the federal government and it may return to the states the functions they can exercise more efficiently. It may at any time that it chooses reassert its power over the purse. It may adopt a new and truthful concept of the public welfare. In an age of personal government we need not despair of a rule of law—and so of liberty—if our legislators will but respect the essential wisdom of the doctrine of the separation of powers. As matters now stand the responsibilities of the Congress are as great in internal affairs as those of the President are in international relations.

III

JUDICIAL DEFERENCE AS A GRAVE CAUSE OF CONSTITUTIONAL IMBALANCE

"T HE judiciary," said the *Federalist,* "is beyond comparison the weakest of the three departments of power ... [It] has no influence over either the sword or the purse; no direction either of the strength or of the wealth of the society; and can take no active resolution whatever. It may truly be said to have neither FORCE nor WILL, but merely judgment." [1] Even Montesquieu, himself a judge and particularly interested in the place of the courts in government, conceded, as he reflected on the government of England in 1748, that "Of the three powers ... the judiciary is in some measure next to nothing." [2] But if Montesquieu realized the relative weakness of the judiciary at the time he wrote, it is evidence of his vision that he appreciated the supreme importance of its independence. "There is no liberty," he said, "if the judiciary

---

[1] Hamilton, *The Federalist No. 78* in *The Federalist, op. cit.,* 502, 504.
[2] *Op. cit.,* Bk. XI, c. VI, par. 32 (p. 178 in I Nugent).

power be not separated from the legislative and executive." [3] This concept is the heart of his great contribution to political philosophy.

It is difficult for us today to realize quite how weak the judicial branch once was and why, for example, John Jay should prefer to be governor of New York to being chief justice of the United States. The judiciary owes its place in American government in large measure to its having been established in our federal and state constitutions in accordance with the doctrine of separation of powers as an independent, coordinate branch of government, and also in part to its being so often called on (in contrast with the English and French judiciary, though for different reasons in each of these countries) to decide what is the "supreme Law of the land" and thus on occasion to override legislative or executive action. Because of this high responsibility the independence of the judiciary from both the legislative and executive branches of government is the keystone of American constitutional government by which we seek to uphold both our national security and individual freedom. That keystone may be impaired or even destroyed by (1) legislative encroachments, (2) executive interference or (3) judicial inaction. I shall consider these three possible sources of danger to the judiciary in that order.

No better example may be found of the dynamic nature of the doctrine of separation of powers than its persuasive influence in overcoming the tradition, inherited from colonial times, of direct legislative intrusion into judicial affairs. The sovereignty of Parliament in England, moreover, was a potent example to American legislatures, even though everyone understood thoroughly that sovereignty here was not vested in any one branch of government. Although their constitutional position was clearly limited,

[3] *Id.,* par. 5 (p. 174 in I Nugent).

legislatures liked to think of themselves as peculiarly the representatives of the sovereign people and thus, by a common species of political reasoning, sovereigns themselves. The period from the Revolution to the Civil War was clearly the heyday of the legislative arm of government in both the states and the nation. We find state legislatures by special act annulling or reversing judgments,[4] granting new trials after final judgment in the courts,[5] giving the right to appeal after the time to do so had expired,[6] probating wills after their rejection by the courts,[7] dictating details of the administration of particular estates,[8] validating specified marriages that were invalid under the general law,[9] suspending the statute of limitations for individual litigants,[10] designating the particular cases to be heard at the next term,[11] empowering the sale of the estates of decedents, infants or incompetents in situations not permitted under the general law,[12] foreclosing mortgages [13] and awarding dower to particular widows.[14]

[4] Act to Reverse Matter of Dorr, 3 R.I. 299 (1854); Bondy *op. cit.*, 99; Pound, *The Formative Era of American Law* 39 (New York, 1950).

[5] *Calder v. Bull*, 3 Dall. 386 (U.S. 1798); *Merrill v. Sherburne*, 1 N.H. 199 (1818); Plumer, William Jr., *Life of William Plumer* 170-171 (Boston, 1857).

[6] *Staniford v. Barry*, 1 Aikens 314, 15 Am. Dec. 691 (Vt. 1826); Bondy, *op. cit.*, 98-99, citing cases declaring act invalid; Smith, E. Fitch, *Commentaries on Statute and Constitutional Law* 523 (Albany, 1848), citing cases holding act unconstitutional.

[7] *Calder v. Bull, op. cit.*

[8] *Leland v. Wilkinson*, 6 Pet. 317, 319 (U.S. 1832).

[9] *Local Laws of Indiana*, 1842, c. 140, p. 130.

[10] *Holden v. James*, 11 Mass. 396, 6 Am. Dec. 174 (1814); Smith, *op. cit.*, 517-518.

[11] Bond, *The Court of Appeals of Maryland* 133 (Baltimore, 1928).

[12] *Rice v. Parkman*, 16 Mass. 326 (1820); I Cooley, *A Treatise on Constitutional Limitations* 194-200 (8th ed., Boston, 1927).

[13] Bondy, *op. cit.*, 94, noting decision against validity of the act.

[14] *Id.*, noting invalidity of the act.

The practice of obtaining new trials from the legislature was the most common of these violations by the legislative branch of the separation of powers. Plumer has described the process in New Hampshire:

> Under the colonial government an appeal was allowed from the ordinary tribunals, in certain cases, to the governor and council. During the revolution, the same practice of going beyond the courts of law for redress was continued; and the form which it took, under the constitution of 1784, was that of a special act of the Legislature, "restoring the party to his law," as it was called, that is, giving him a new trial in the Superior Court, after his case had come to its final decision in the ordinary course of law.[15]

He narrates how his father succeeded in 1791 in having the New Hampshire court declare such a special act unconstitutional. Commenting on this decision he says:

> But though it required some courage in the attorney to take the exception, and more, perhaps, in the court to sustain it, the good sense of the people acquiesced in the decision. Some clamor was indeed made against the judges, as putting themselves above the Legislature; and attempts were made at subsequent sessions, generally without success, by disappointed litigants to get laws passed granting them new trials. In 1817, such a law was passed; but the Superior Court, in an elaborate opinion, pronounced it unconstitutional. No attempt has been since made to reverse this decision.[16]

The practice continued in Rhode Island until 1856 when the highest court in the state said bluntly, "It is quite evident, too, that this distribution of powers was, in our constitution, made for the special purpose of depriving the general assembly of their long

---

[15] Plumer, *op. cit.,* 170.
[16] *Id.,* 171.

exercised judicial power, which, rightly or wrongly, that body had assumed under the charter."[17] The practice of legislative interference with the work of the courts lingered on until the adoption of the Fourteenth Amendment.

Legislative divorces were another anomaly that too long cast their shadow over American justice. Sometimes these legislative acts of divorce in individual cases were passed after a hearing by a legislative committee and on its recommendation but without full knowledge by the entire legislature, and sometimes they were passed without any hearing of the parties at all. In every instance they were granted not as a matter of right to the petitioner but as a matter of legislative grace. In such circumstances it was impossible to hope for equal treatment for all. It is difficult to conceive of any subject on which the legislature was less qualified or more poorly organized to adjudicate, yet as late as 1887 legislative divorces in the territories of the United States were upheld by the Supreme Court,[18] a year after the Congress had taken away that power from the territorial legislatures.[19] Cooley is conservative when he says that "the general sentiment in the legal profession is against the rightfulness of special legislative divorces."[20] They likewise offended the popular sense of justice. By 1882, thirty states,[21] and by 1938, forty states had constitutional provisions against legislative divorces. The remaining states have taken care

[17] *Taylor & Co. v. Place,* 4 R.I. 324, 348-349 (1856).

[18] *Maynard v. Hill,* 125 U.S. 190, 208-209 (1887).

[19] Frankfurter and Davison, *Cases and Materials on Administrative Law* 30 (2d ed., Chicago, 1935), citing Act of July 30, 1886, 24 Stat. 170, c. 818; I Bishop, *New Commentaries on Marriage, Divorce, and Separation* 71 (Chicago, 1891).

[20] Cooley, *op. cit.,* 212.

[21] Noble, *The Marriage and Divorce Laws of the United States* 55 (New York, 1882).

of the problem by other constitutional provisions or statutes, with the exception of Connecticut, Maine, Rhode Island and Vermont, where the legislative divorce has been so discredited that there is no likelihood of its revival even in the absence of a constitutional amendment or a statute.[22] As Chief Justice Simeon E. Baldwin said, "The whole drift of modern institutions is away from unconfined legislative power. The grant of legislative divorce is one of the extremest forms which it can assume. It does not belong to the social life of the twentieth century."[23]

Some legislative attempts at interference with the work of the courts still persist. Declaratory acts seeking to interpret earlier legislation and to give the interpretation retroactive effect are generally condemned. It is interesting to note the contrast between the rule here and the rule in England, where, because of the supremacy of Parliament and the absence of separation of powers in the American sense, declaratory legislation is given retroactive effect when the language so warrants.[24] Curative or validating legislation, moreover, still troubles our courts when in effect it interferes with judicial determinations.[25] The trend of the decisions is to uphold such a curative or validating act even

[22] II Vernier, *American Family Laws* § 64, 14-18 (Stanford, 1932). No changes were reported in the 1938 Supplement to this volume.

[23] Baldwin, *Legislative Divorces and the Fourteenth Amendment,* 27 Harv. L. Rev. 699, 704 (1914).

[24] Wade and Phillips, *Constitutional Law* 38-39 (4th ed. London, 1950).

[25] See for example, *Wilcox v. Miner,* 201 Iowa 476, 205 N. W. 847 (1925) where a statute cured a defect in the tax law and a court injunction preventing the county treasurer from collecting the tax was vacated. But see *People v. Clark,* 300 Ill. 583, 133 N.E. 247 (1921), where the court refused to give effect to a curative act which attempted to remove restrictions against one from holding a position on a school board, saying that the court would apply the law as it existed and would not reverse its ouster.

though it impairs or renders ineffective a judgment if it concerns a public right, but to declare it void when it affects a private right.[26]

Another survival of legislative justice that does no credit to our jurisprudence is the settlement of claims against the state by legislative enactment rather than by suit in court, a situation due to the continued acceptance in many states of the outmoded doctrine of the immunity from liability of the sovereign state and often of its political subdivisions, the American equivalent of the equally outmoded English doctrine that the king can do no wrong.[27] The doctrine works increasing hardship in an age of expanding governmental activities.

A further source of conflict between the legislature and the courts concerns the power to control admissions to the bar. It is beyond question that the courts could not function without the aid of the bar, and accordingly the members of the bar are deemed to be officers of the courts. The power of the courts therefore to control the admission of lawyers to practice and their conduct after admission goes to the heart of the administration of justice.[28] The authority of the courts to discipline attorneys for misconduct is generally conceded,[29] but in some states the legis-

[26] 11 *Am. Juris.* § 212 (1951 Supp.).

[27] Pound, *Justice According to Law,* 14 Col. L. Rev. 1, 3 (1914).

[28] *People v. Goodman,* 366 Ill. 346, 8 N.E. 2d 941, *cert. denied, Goodman v. Illinois,* 302 U.S. 728, 58 S. Ct. 49, *rehearing denied,* 302 U.S. 777, 58 S. Ct. 138 (1937); *In re Opinion of the Justices,* 279 Mass. 607, 180 N.E. 725 (1932); Bruce, *The Judicial Prerogative and Admission to the Bar,* 19 Ill. I. Rev. 1 (1924); Cheadle, *Inherent Power of the Judiciary Over Admittance to the Bar,* 7 Wash. L. Rev. 318 (1932); 3 Vand. L. Rev. 116 (1949).

[29] *In re Bruen,* 102 Wash. 472, 172 Pac. 1152 (1918); *People v. Gulkin,* 248 N.Y. 465, 162 N.E. 487 (1928); *In re Richards,* 333 Mo. 907, 63 S.W. 2d 672 (1933); Cheadle, *id.,* 330-332; Shanfeld, *The Scope of Judicial Inde-*

lature still claims the power to regulate admissions to the bar,[30] and in a few more the courts, while holding that the power of admission is judicial in nature, acquiesce in the legislative prescription of regulations, if reasonable.[31] There is no more justification for a legislature controlling admissions to the bar than there would be for the courts adjudicating on the qualifications of members of a legislature or of its employees, and fortunately that is the view taken in the majority of the states.[32]

Closely related to the problem of admissions to the bar is the question of laymen practicing before administrative agencies. The Supreme Court has held[33] that the question is one for the Congress, which has delegated power in the matter to the administrative agencies concerned. This means that in the federal field the courts have been rendered powerless to deal with the problem, hence the need for legislation such as is now pending before Congress.[34] In the states, on the other hand, the courts have dealt with the problem. Generally they have held that they have inherent

pendence of the Legislature in Matters of Procedure and Control of the Bar, 19 St. Louis L. Rev. 163 (1934).

[30] In re Applicants for License, 143 N.C. 1, 55 S.E. 635 (1906); Matter of Cooper, 22 N.Y. 67 (1860); 144 A.L.R. 150, 152-153; 25 Notre Dame Law. 143 (1949).

[31] In re Opinion of the Justices, op. cit.; State v. Cannon, 206 Wis. 374, 240 N.W. 441 (1932); In re Day, 81 Ill. 73, 54 N.E. 646 (1899); 144 A.L.R. 150.

[32] Application of Kaufman, 69 Idaho 297, 209 P. 2d 528 (1949); State ex rel. Ralston v. Turner, 141 Neb. 556, 4 N.W. 2d 302 (1942); Shanfeld, op. cit.; 25 Notre Dame Law., op. cit.; 8 Geo. Wash. Law Rev. 1085 (1940).

[33] Goldsmith v. Board of Tax Appeals, 270 U.S. 117, 46 S. Ct. 215 (1926).

[34] H. R. 2657, 80th Cong., 1st Sess. (1947). Bill reintroduced in March, 1951, H.R. 3097, 82d Cong., 1st Sess. (1951), and sent to House Judiciary Committee. For discussion, see 48 Col. L. Rev. 120 (1948).

power to prevent the unauthorized practice of law[35] and that the appearance of laymen before administrative tribunals is such unauthorized practice.[36]

Another ground of vigorous conflict between the legislative and judicial branches of government concerns the right of the courts to promulgate rules governing their procedure and practice. On principle the question would seem to be governed by the same considerations as admissions to the bar. One would not expect the courts to be called upon to adjudicate contests as to the seating or expulsion of members of the legislature even though they are most decidedly controversies, and by the same token one would not expect the legislature to prescribe the rules of procedure to govern the operation of the judicial branch of government. Practice and procedure in the courts were originally matters of custom, yet rules of court were utilized to effect improvements in procedure as far back as the middle ages. With the single exception of the original Field Code all of the great improvements in judicial procedure over the centuries, as the law has moved forward from trial by ordeal and trial by battle to its relatively rational basis today, have been by judicial action, generally in the form of rules of court. That rules of court did not continue to be the exclusive means of developing practice and procedure is attributable in England to the development of parliamentary su-

---

[35] *Matter of New York County Lawyers Ass'n (Bercu).* 270 App. Div. 524 (1948), *aff'd,* 299 N.Y. 728 (1949); *Fitchette v. Taylor,* 191 Minn. 582, 254 N.W. 910 (1934); Brand, *Unauthorized Practice Decisions* (Detroit, 1937); Otterbourg, *A Study of Unauthorized Practice of Law,* Unauthorized Practice News (Special Ed., Sept., 1951).

[36] *Stack v. P. G. Garage, Inc.* 7 N.J. 118 (1951); *State v. Childe,* 147 Neb. 527, 23 N.W. 2d 720 (1946); *State v. Wills,* 191 S.C. 468, 5 S.E. 2d 181 (1939); *People v. Goodman, op. cit.;* 35 Mich. L. Rev. 442 (1937).

premacy and its effect for a time on the English courts. In this country it was due, first, to the dominance of the legislative branch down to the Civil War; second, to the preoccupation of the profession with the monumental task of adapting our public and private substantive law to the needs of a new country; and, finally, to the effects on the entire field of procedural law of the equalitarian movement of the second quarter of the nineteenth century. In most states this movement resulted in judges being elected for short terms on the principle of rotation in office;[37] in the muzzling of the trial judge by precluding him from interrogating witnesses, from commenting on or summarizing the evidence, and from charging the jury except in the language of the instructions submitted to him by counsel rather than in words of his own choosing.[38] These factors made possible, indeed necessitated the simple Field Code of Civil Procedure of a century ago—and I emphasize the word simple because the original Field Code was simple. Then, too, the tendency of that era to view the doctrine of the separation of powers analytically rather than historically or functionally strengthened the view that rule-making was legislative in nature despite the experience of previous centuries to the contrary. The Field Code, like every other procedural code, however, was subject to the inherent weakness that it was susceptible to perennial and multitudinous amendments, many of them passed to overcome the supposed defects of the code in individual cases. The code, too, had the defect of all legislation in being rigid and inflexible as compared with the elasticity and adaptability of rules of court. In many states, therefore, the codes of procedure have

[37] Vanderbilt, *Minimum Standards of Judicial Administration* xxiii, 270 (New York, 1949).

[38] *Id.*, 221-234.

in the course of a century become far worse than the medieval maze that they superseded.[39]

From this brief recital of the course of procedural history in this country, however, it must not be thought that all the courts abdicated their power to make rules governing practice and procedure. In 1792 we find Chief Justice Jay stating that the Supreme Court of the United States "considers the practice of the courts of *King's Bench* and *Chancery* in *England,* as affording outlines for the practice of this court; and that they will, from time to time, make such alterations therein, as circumstances may render necessary." [40] The federal courts have led the way in the development of modern rule-making; first, in 1842 with equity and admirality rules, then, in 1898 with bankruptcy procedure, in 1938 with rules of civil procedure, and in 1946 with rules of criminal procedure.

The modern trend throughout the country has been to give the courts the power to regulate their own procedure and administration and then to hold them responsible for results.[41] The reasons for this trend are obvious. Rules of court are made by experts who are familiar with the specific problems to be solved and the various ways of solving them. Preliminary drafts of the rules can and should be submitted prior to promulgation to the scrutiny of the entire bench and bar for their criticisms and suggestions. This was the practice pursued in the formulation of the Federal Rules of Civil and Criminal Procedure. In New Jersey we have not only followed the federal example, but each year we have a two-day conference of judges and lawyers, of legislative leaders and representative laymen, for the purpose of making recommendations for

[39] Pound, *David Dudley Field: An Appraisal, David Dudley Field Centenary Essays* 3 (New York, 1949); Clark, *Code Pleading and Practice Today, David Dudley Field Centenary Essays, id.,* 55.

[40] *Hayburn's Case,* 2 Dall. 409, 413-414 (U.S. 1792).

[41] Vanderbilt, *op. cit.,* 91-145.

the improvement of the rules in the light of the year's experience.[42] The rule-making process must be a continuous one if stagnation is to be avoided. Changes may be made whenever the need is felt without waiting for stated legislative sessions and without burdening already overworked legislators. Rules of court, moreover, have the great advantage that not only are they made by experts, but they are interpreted and applied by judges who are sympathetic with them. By judicial rule-making procedure may be made subsidiary, as it should be, to a consideration of the substantial rights of the litigants, enabling the courts to avoid the snarls of procedural red tape that are all too often found in codes of procedure and to concentrate on the substantive questions at issue.

The case for judicial rule-making has never been better stated than by Dean Pound and Dean Wigmore a quarter of a century ago.[43] It was largely their teaching and the dissatisfaction of the bench and bar with complicated codes of civil procedure that led in 1938 to the unanimous adoption by the American Bar Association of the recommendation:

That practice and procedure in the courts should be regulated by rules of court; and that to this end the courts should be given full rule-making powers.

The bar recognizes that rule-making power is essential to the courts if they are to be truly independent and if the balance of power intended by the Constitution is to be maintained.

In my second lecture I emphasized the ever-increasing expansion of the federal government. It is important to realize that

[42] Rule 1:7-3, Rules of Practice and Procedure Governing the Courts of New Jersey.
[43] Pound, *The Rule-Making Power of the Courts,* 12 A.B.A.J. 599 (1926); Wigmore, *All Legislative Rules for Judiciary Procedure Are Void Constitutionally,* 23 Ill. L. Rev. 276 (1928).

this trend toward centralization in Washington operates not only to destroy the balance of power between the state and federal governments, but also to disturb the balance between the three branches of government at the expense of the judiciary. Let me illustrate how this process works. Traditionally in this country the relations between an employer and his employees have been a matter of exclusively local concern. The rights of each as against the other were governed primarily by common-law rules of contract and of master and servant. When disputes arose between them, either party had recourse to the state courts to vindicate his rights and the state courts had full power to grant such legal or equitable relief as the circumstances warranted. In the performance of their judicial functions the state courts were free from legislative or executive interference, for generally the state constitutions prescribe the jurisdiction of the courts of general jurisdiction and thus preclude any reduction in their powers by the legislature. This situation was changed, however, when, under broad interpretations of the commerce clause of the Constitution, the Congress entered the field of labor-management relations with the result that the jurisdiction of the states has been gradually reduced until today it has almost been eliminated.[44] This shift in jurisdiction over labor relations from the states to the federal government was accompanied by a reduction in the power of the judiciary to protect the rights of the parties. This was so because of the fact that, unlike most state courts, the jurisdiction of the federal courts, except the original jurisdiction of the Supreme Court, has been held to be subject to legislative control and the Congress has not hesitated to impose such jurisdictional restrictions as it deems the

[44] *Bus Employees v. Wisconsin Board,* 340 U.S. 383, 71 S. Ct. 359 (1951); *Norris Grain Co. v. Nordaas,* 232 Minn. 91, 46 N.W. 2d 94 (1950); 174 A.L.R. 1051.

exigencies of particular situations require. In this way the ability of individuals to resort to either the state or federal courts to vindicate their rights has been substantially reduced and the power of the judiciary to afford protection and relief considerably impaired.

An outstanding example of this process is the Norris-La Guardia Act, passed in 1932,[45] the stated purpose of which was "to define and limit the jurisdiction of courts sitting in equity, and for other purposes." [46] There was considerable discussion at the time as to the act's constitutionality in view of section 2 of Article III of the Constitution. Section 1 of this article, it will be recalled, provides: "The judicial Power of the United States, shall be vested in one supreme Court and in such inferior Courts as the Congress may from time to time ordain and establish." Standing alone, this would give the Congress power to fix the jurisdiction of such courts as it might establish, but section 2 states: "The judicial power shall extend to all Cases, in Law and Equity" and opponents of this legislation contended that the "power to restrain by injunction is inherent in equity courts and is of the very essence of the power" and that the legislature could not "so impinge upon their inherent equity powers by any regulation of their procedure as to destroy altogether the power of the court to vindicate its existence and discharge its exalted functions." [47] Their arguments were of little avail, however, for the Supreme Court had long since taken the position that the jurisdiction of the federal courts was subject to congressional control. In *Ex parte McCardle*[48]

[45] 47 Stat. 70-73 (1932), 29 U.S.C. §§ 101-115 (1946).

[46] Act of Congress of March 23, 1932, c. 90, § 1, 47 Stat. 70 (1932).

[47] From the speech of Representative James M. Beck in the House of Representatives on March 8, 1932 as quoted in Editorial, 18 A.B.A.J. 248, 249 (1932).

[48] 74 U.S. 506 (1869); see also *Kline v. Burke Construction Co.*, 260

the Supreme Court sustained an act of Congress, passed in its conflict with President Johnson over reconstruction, depriving the Supreme Court of jurisdiction to decide certain appeals, among them being McCardle's which had already been argued before it. Accordingly, when the question of the constitutionality of the anti-injunction provisions of the Norris-La Guardia Act was presented to it, the Supreme Court found little difficulty in sustaining the power of Congress to limit the equity jurisdiction of the federal trial courts.[49] The Act is but one example of how the Congress may remove a subject of vital importance from the province of the states and the state courts and then, in the exercise of its power over the federal courts, restrict or eliminate the right of persons directly concerned to secure the relief that the courts were designed to afford them. The Emergency Price Control Act discussed in Lecture II is another striking illustration of congressional limitations on resort to the courts and of restrictions on their traditional powers. If the Congress can interfere with the injunctive process on the one hand and substantially impair the right of a defendant to contest the validity of the law he is accused of violating on the other, one might well ask whether there is any limit to congressional interference with the courts.

Another wide field of legislative action in derogation of the powers of the judiciary is to be found in the creation of administrative agencies endowed with the right to make determinations in matters which had traditionally been within the jurisdiction of the courts.[50] To the extent that the states have resorted to the use

U.S. 226, 43 S. Ct. 79 (1922); *Sheldon v. Sill*, 8 How. (49 U.S.) 441 (1850); *Cary v. Curtis*, 3 How. (44 U.S.) 236 (1845).

[49] *New Negro Alliance v. Grocery Co.*, 303 U.S. 552 (1938), opinion amended 304 U.S. 542 (1938); *Lauf v. E. G. Shinner & Co.*, 303 U.S. 323, 58 S. Ct. 578 (1938).

[50] Brown, *Administrative Commissions and the Judicial Power*, 19 Minn.

of such administrative tribunals for adjudication, the business of the state courts has been substantially reduced, but not their powers because of the constitutional right of an individual to secure a review of administrative determinations through the great prerogative writs or their modern substitutes even in circumstances where the legislature may not have provided for review.[51] The powers of the federal courts, on the other hand, have been substantially reduced in controversies coming up from federal administrative agencies, because the extent of the review accorded by the Congress or provided by the federal courts in the absence of statute[52] may be and often is less efficacious than the review afforded by the state courts.[53] Thus, the increase in the number and scope of activities of federal administrative tribunals has served to decrease the power not only of the states themselves, but of the state and federal judiciary as well. In the light of these developments it would seem desirable to reconsider the question of congressional control over the jurisdiction of the federal judiciary and, if it be deemed advisable, to amend the judicial section of the Federal Constitution so as to preserve the fundamental right of individuals to resort to the courts for relief.

L. Rev. 261, 266 (1935); Powell, *Separation of Powers: Administrative Exercise of Legislative and Judicial Power,* 27 Pol. Sci. Q. 215, 234 (1912); Pound, *Executive Justice,* 55 U. of Pa. L. Rev. 137, 139 (1907).

[51] *Louisiana & Nash. R. R. Co. v. Garrett,* 231 U.S. 298, 310-311, 34 S. Ct. 48, 53 (1913); *Foster v. Goodpaster,* 290 Ky. 410, 161 S.W. 2d 626 (1942); *Cofman v. Ousterhous,* 40 N.D. 390, 402, 168 N.W. 826, 829 (1918); *Sabre v. Rutland R. R. Co.,* 86 Vt. 347, 366-369, 85 Atl. 693, 701-702 (1913).

[52] *Estep v. United States,* 327 U.S. 114, 66 S. Ct. 423 (1946); *Stark v. Wickard,* 321 U.S. 288, 64 S. Ct. 559 (1944).

[53] Vanderbilt, *Administrative Law, 1944 Annual Survey of American Law* 169, 205-213 (N.Y.U. School of Law, 1946).

The state legislatures havé not only interfered with judicial functions in the various ways we have outlined; they have long cast many nonjudicial duties on the judiciary. This has traditionally been the practice in England both at the county level and nationally, and it was carried over to the colonies[54] and then to the states despite statements in the constitutions of many states expressly setting up the principle of the separation of powers. Dean Pound has cataloged a wide variety of the nonjudicial functions of an eighteenth-century judge:

In Connecticut, the County Courts appointed Collectors of Excise. In New York, the justices of the peace had a duty of building and repairing jails and court houses and of raising money for that purpose. In New Jersey, the Court of Quarter Sessions granted tavern licenses and recommended peddlers and heard appeals from assessors, while single justices could discharge apprentices or provide punishment of them, subject to appeal to the sessions. In Pennsylvania, the Quarter Sessions licensed rangers to take up stray cattle, had jurisdiction of appeals from assessment of highway taxes, appointed highway supervisors and trustees of the house of correction, appointed and removed the keeper and employees of the house of correction, audited the accounts of treasurers of lotteries, and made orders as to imported vagrants. In Delaware, the Quarter Sessions regulated the baking, and size, and weight of loaves of bread, and justices of the peace sat with the grand jurymen and assessors to levy taxes, appointed the keepers of work houses, administered the poor laws subject to appeal to the Quarter Sessions, and appointed constables. In Maryland, the County Courts had a general administrative jurisdiction. So it was in Virginia, where those courts regulated public utilities. For example, they licensed ferry keepers and prescribed the re-

---

[54] Pound, *Organization of Courts* 5-6 (Boston, 1940); Dodd, *State Government* 64 (2d ed., New York, 1928); Goebel, *King's Law and Local Custom in Seventeenth Century New England,* 31 Col. L. Rev. 416 (1931).

quired facilities and established public warehouses for tobacco. In North Carolina, the justices of the peace levied taxes, divided counties into districts, appointed road commissioners, ordered the laying out of roads, established ferries, appointed where bridges should be built, and under special statutes levied taxes to build court houses, prisons, and stocks. In South Carolina, the County and Precinct Courts, afterwards superseded by the General Court, had general administrative powers. So had the justices of the peace in Georgia.[55]

Throughout the country the situation has not changed. In most jurisdictions the nonjudicial duties of the modern judge are even more extensive than in colonial times. A cursory examination of the laws of a single state discloses that its judges are called upon to appoint county park commissioners, water commissioners, morgue keepers, commissioners to survey the boundaries between municipalities, and persons to examine maimed, sick or disabled animals. They have been designated as members of the board of trustees of the county parental school and of the board of review for the classification and reclassification of bidders on public contracts. They are empowered by statute to issue permits to sell pistols and revolvers at retail, to issue permits to purchase pistols and revolvers, to issue permits "after investigation" to carry concealed firearms and also to revoke such permits, and to issue permits for the purchase and possession of machine guns and automatic rifles. They are required to investigate whether or not a municipality has defaulted on its notes and if so to file an order on the basis of which the municipal finance commission shall exercise its statutory powers, to report to the muncipalities with regard to any degrading conditions found existing therein, to organize clinics for the study of the physical and mental condition of

[55] *Organization of Courts, op. cit.,* 88-89; see also *Village of Saratoga Springs v. Saratoga Co.,* 191 N.Y. 123 (1908).

criminal defendants and to aid corporations for the prevention of cruelty to children. They are authorized to perform marriage ceremonies. They are directed to certify the clipping of the ears of fox and woodchuck and to issue bounty certificates therefor; and in the absence of the coroner to hold inquests in cases of suspicious deaths. Various statutory proceedings are committed by the legislature to the courts, of which transfer inheritance tax proceedings and applications for the recount of votes following an election are typical examples.[56] The situation in this one state may be duplicated or even amplified in almost any other state. Even the federal government calls on the state judges to aid in naturalization matters.[57]

The delegation to the courts by the legislature of nonjudicial duties reflects an instinctive desire to seek an impartial and independent tribunal for the handling of a wide variety of matters deemed vital to the welfare of the community. It is to be observed, moreover, that the courts have not tolerated in legislative delegation of nonjudicial powers to the judiciary any attempt to make the courts subservient to or under the supervision of either the legislative or executive branch. One of the earliest cases to come before the Supreme Court of the United States involved a statute which cast on the Supreme Court justices while riding circuit the duty of passing on pensions for invalided Revolutionary soldiers, subject to the consideration and suspension of any pensions so granted by the secretary of war and to their revision by the Congress. Such executive and legislative review was deemed incompatible with the unfettered nature of judicial powers. The

[56] *Massett Building Co. v. Bennett,* 4 N.J. 53, 59-60, 71 A. 2d 327, 330-331 (1950).

[57] 54 Stat. 1140 (1940), 8 U.S.C. § 701 (1946); Baldwin, *The American Judiciary* 134, 153 (New York, 1905); Bondy, *op. cit.,* 176.

justices on circuit declined to act on the pension claims submitted to them, and an appeal therefrom was not pressed to a conclusion.[58] Similarly, a New York statute casting on a justice of its Supreme Court the mandatory duty of investigating charges against a public official and reporting the evidence with his findings and conclusions to the governor was held unconstitutional.[59] The work of a judge cannot be made subject to the supervision of another branch of the government if the judicial department is to remain independent. Nor can a judge be obliged to carry out any legislative grant of nonjudicial authority if it interferes with his judicial work, either by taking too much of his time and attention[60] or by involving him in situations that may reflect on his reputation in the community for independence or for freedom from politics.[61] Where any of these factors exist, judges have not hesitated to decline nonjudicial responsibilities. In general it may be stated that the courts have been much more inclined to uphold the delegation of legislative power to part-time justices of the peace, who often act on the governing boards of towns, a tradition inherited from England, and to rural county courts that in so many respects resemble the quarter sessions of England with their judicial and administrative duties, than they have similar delegation to judges of courts of general trial or appellate jurisdiction.

There is no sound principle in our constitutions underlying this distinction, however, for the judge of a county court and a

[58] *Hayburn's Case, op. cit.*

[59] *In re Richardson,* 247 N.Y. 401, 160 N.E. 655 (1928).

[60] Voss, *Exercise of Non-Judicial Functions by Courts and Judges,* 7 Kan. Bar Bull. 172, 179 (1939).

[61] *State ex rel. White v. Barker,* 116 Iowa 69, 89 N.W. 204 (1902); Shelton, *Spirit of the Courts,* 235-236 (Baltimore, 1918); Spilman, 2 Kan. L.J. 57, 58 (1885), as cited in *Sartin v. Snell,* 87 Kan. 485, 125 Pac. 47 (1912).

justice of the peace have as much responsibility and, indeed, much greater opportunity for building up popular respect for law on which in the last analysis democratic government must rest than has the judge of a court of general jurisdiction or an appellate judge with whom people generally come far less in contact. All judges should, on principle, confine their attention to judicial work. Especially should this be done in courts that are over-burdened and behind with their work. The public finds it difficult to understand why a judge should assume nonjudicial duties when he has not yet fulfilled his judicial responsibilities. Just as the legislative branch owes an obligation to the public to strengthen its resources and machinery to meet the increasing power of the executive in legislative matters, so the judges owe it to the public and to themselves to decline, with rare exceptions, to exercise legislatively conferred nonjudicial tasks.

Closely related to the matter we have been discussing is the practice of the executive in calling on judges to perform special tasks in the executive branch of government, often tasks of an investigatory or controversial nature. In 1947 the Senate Commit-tee on the Judiciary filed a report[62] listing eleven instances in the few years between 1942 and 1947 when federal judges, two of them Supreme Court justices, were employed on such missions by the chief executive, although Chief Justice Stone refused the chair-manship of the Atomic Energy Commission and membership on the United States Ballot Commission, just as Mr. Justice Cardozo, when chief judge of the New York Court of Appeals, had de-clined appointment to the International Court of Justice.[63] The

[62] Reprinted in 33 A.B.A.J. 792 (1947).

[63]   "Sept. 8, 1927

"My dear Judge Hughes:

"On the eve of your departure to Europe we had a conference on the

committee report in condemning the practice lists five undesirable results which may flow from the use of judges on executive missions:

(1) Reward may be conferred or expected in the form of elevation to a higher judicial post.
(2) The judicial and executive functions may be improperly merged.
(3) The absence of the judge from his regular duties increases the work load of the other judges of the court, if any, and may result in an impairment of judicial efficiency in the disposition of cases.

subject of my proposed membership in the Permanent Court of Arbitration at The Hague. I promised to recur to the subject on your return.

"After many inward struggles I have come to the conclusion that a Judge of the Court of Appeals best serves the people of the State by refusing to assume an obligation that in indeterminate, if improbable, contingencies might take precedence of the obligations attached to his judicial office.

"The Constitution of the State excludes a Judge of the Court of Appeals or a Justice of the Supreme Court from holding any other office or public trust. In my opinion, membership in the Court of Arbitration is not an office or a public trust within that prohibition. Analysis of the constitution of the Hague Tribunal is necessary, however, before this conclusion becomes obvious. To the minds of many, I might seem, in accepting membership, to be violating the letter of the command of the Constitution, or to be making nice distinctions to win an honor for myself. Even if I were to make it clear that membership does not violate the letter of the mandate there might be many who would feel that there had been an offense against the spirit. I think I shall best maintain the dignity and fair fame of the great office that I hold if I avoid the occasion and the possibility of debate or misconstruction. None more fully than you will feel an understanding sympathy for this attitude of mind.

"I am grateful to the President for his generous confidence. Though I put honor aside, it is with many a pang of regret and in obedience to a sense of duty. Every impulse of personal desire would move me to another choice." As contained in Frankfurter and Davison, *op. cit.,* 326-327.

(4) Nonjudicial activities may produce dissension or criticism and may be destructive of the prestige and respect of the federal judicary.

(5) A judge, upon resumption of his regular duties, may be called upon to justify or defend his activities under an executive commission.[64]

Notwithstanding this warning in the report of the committee of prohibitory legislation, the President recently endeavored to enlist the services of Judge Thomas F. Murphy of the United States District Court for the Southern District of New York for conducting the highly controversial investigation of corruption in the federal government, but the judge on the advice of his colleagues declined.[65] It is interesting to note that Mr. Justice Jackson, who acted on presidential appointment as chief counsel for the United States in the prosecution of Axis war criminals at Nuremberg during the entire 1945-1946 term of the Supreme Court, is quoted as being "of the personal view that members of the Supreme Court should be made ineligible to hold any other office or appointment under the Government of the United States, so far as such designations will be for the performance of duties which are administrative or nonjudicial in character or which involve the laws or domestic affairs of the United States or the performance of duty by other public officers." [66]

The undesirable practice herein referred to is not of recent origin. Chief Justice Jay went to England in 1795 to negotiate the treaty that bears his name and Chief Justice Ellsworth went to France in 1799 to negotiate an agreement with Napoleon. Each was given a diplomatic appointment confirmed by the Senate

[64] 33 A.B.A.J., *op. cit.*, 795.

[65] N. Y. *Times,* Dec. 22, 1951, p. 1, col. 4; N. Y. *Times,* Dec. 23, 1951, p. 1, col. 7.

[66] As reported in 32 A.B.A.J. 862-863 (1946).

and each continued to hold the office of chief justice during an absence of more than a year, but these appointments were accepted at a time when the work of the court was nominal and before the government had grown to the proportions of the present day. John Marshall served as Secretary of War for a month after taking the oath of office of chief justice. Chief Justice Fuller, however, declined President Cleveland's invitation to become Secretary of State on the ground that his resignation in the circumstances would be "distinctly injurious to the Court." Mr. Justice Bradley served on the Electoral Commission in the disputed Hayes-Tilden election of 1876; his decisive vote in favor of Hayes, a Republican, aroused much criticism because of the fact that he, too, was a Republican. When judges accept nonjudicial duties at the behest of the executive, they do so as a matter of judicial deference, of which more will be said later, rather than because of any obligation to accept such appointments.

The delegation by the legislature of nonjudicial power to judges has been paralleled, inconsistently in principle, in many states by an even more extensive grant of judicial powers to officials in the executive arm of the government. This was traditional in England and the practice was carried over here,[67] just as in the case of legislative delegation of nonjudicial powers to judges, notwithstanding the provisions of state constitutions with respect to the doctrine of separation of powers. Thus, in Massachusetts the governor and council were given jurisdiction "in causes of Marriage, divorce and alimony and of probate appeals" until the legisla-

---

[67] Dodd, *State Government, op. cit.,* 64; Greene, *The Provincial Governor in the English Colonies of North America* 110-112, 134-139 (New York, 1898); Labaree, *Royal Government in America* 373-374, 379-380, 403 (New Haven, 1930); Pound, *Organization of Courts, op. cit.,* 56, 59-60; Warren, *A History of the American Bar* 3 (Boston, 1911).

ture provided otherwise.[68] In some states the governor was a member of the court of last resort.[69] In other states appellate jurisdiction was vested in the legislature or a branch thereof, this practice surviving in New York until 1846 and in Rhode Island until 1857.[70] It was the common practice to give the mayors of cities and towns judicial powers,[71] a practice still continued in many rural areas and even, strangely enough, in New York City,[72] where the late Mayor Fiorella La Guardia staged many a colorful demonstration of his prowess as a magistrate in "driving crime from the metropolis."[73] Even the President has been granted such powers. Thus, in the *Runkle* case[74] the Supreme Court recognized the judicial power of President Lincoln to approve or disapprove a decision under the Articles of War of a court martial which in time of peace extended to loss of life or dismissal of a commissioned officer. Equally interesting is the *Whisky* case[75] in which President Taft sat. Regulations issued by the Bureau of Internal Revenue under the Pure Food Act of 1906 had been challenged by interested distillers. The question was the determination of

[68] Mass. Const. c. 3, art. 5 (1780).

[69] Pound, *Organization of Courts, op. cit.,* 96-97.

[70] Aumann, *The Changing American Legal System* 164 (Columbus, 1940).

[71] Dodd, *op. cit.,* 73; Pound, *The Administration of Justice in the Modern City,* 26 Harv. L. Rev. 302 (1913); Woodbridge, *History of Separation of Powers in Ohio,* 13 U. of Cin. L. Rev. 191 (1939).

[72] N. Y. City Charter, c. 1, § 6 (1938).

[73] Limpus and Leyson, *This Man La Guardia* 382 (New York, 1938); N. Y. *Times,* Aug. 18, 1937, p. 42, col. 1; N. Y. *Times,* July 14, 1934, p. 14, col. 1.

[74] *Runkle v. U.S.,* 122 U.S. 543, 7 S. Ct. 1141 (1887).

[75] Proceedings before and by Direction of the President Concerning the Meaning of the Term "Whisky" (1909). See Federal Food and Drug Act Decisions 831 (1914). Opinion also reported in McFarland and Vanderbilt, *Cases on Administrative Law* 575 (New York, 1947).

the meaning of the word "whisky." A rehearing was held before the solicitor general, who submitted a report to President Taft. The distillers appealed from this report and on the appeal the President heard the final argument and rendered the decision, directing the appropriate agencies to prepare regulations in accordance with his opinion. The power of a governor to remove public officers for cause after hearing, pursuant to statute, has likewise been upheld.[76] A motor vehicle commissioner has also been given the powers of a magistrate with respect to the enforcement of the motor vehicle laws.[77]

Nor is the granting of judicial powers confined to single executive officers. Workmen's compensation commissions for adjudicating industrial accidents have been uniformly sustained,[78] and the example has been extended to irrigation statutes for "adjudicating streams"[79] and many other matters. These legislative grants of judicial power in the states are not inconsistent with the principle of the separation of powers. There are many governmental duties which cannot possibly be performed either by the legislature or by the governor and which are certainly not prescribed by the constitution to the judiciary. They lie outside the powers necessarily and properly belonging to the executive, the legis-

[76] McCran v. Gaul, 96 N.J.L. 165, 112 Atl. 603 (1921); Tuttle, Removal of Public Officers for Cause, 3 Mich. L. Rev. 290, 337 (1905).

[77] N.J.S.A. 39:5-2 (1939).

[78] Mulhearn v. Federal Shipbuilding & Dry Dock Co., 2 N.J. 356, 66 A. 2d 726 (1949); State v. Industrial Commission of Ohio, 135 Ohio St. 214, 20 N.E. 2d 248 (1939); Western Metal Supply Co. v. Pillsbury, 172 Cal. 407, 156 Pac. 491 (1916); Hunter v. Colfax Consol. Coal Co., 175 Iowa 245, 154 N.W. 1037 (1915); Diebeikis v. Link-Belt Co., 261 Ill. 454, 104 N.E. 211 (1914).

[79] State v. Knapp, 167 Kan. 546, 207 P. 2d 440 (1949); Burgess v. American Rio Grande Land & Irrigation Co., 295 S.W. 649 (Tex. Civ. App. 1927); Pound, Executive Justice, op. cit., 141.

lative and the judicial departments and may therefore be assigned, as Chief Justice Marshall early pointed out, to such branch as the legislature may think appropriate. All adjudication is not necessarily judicial. For example, when the legislature passes on the qualification of its members or disciplines one of its members, it is adjudicating but it is not performing a judicial function. Aside from such legislative adjudications, however, all adjudication may be taken to the courts under some form or other of judicial review and accordingly the doctrine of the separation of powers has not been infringed.

Tension between the chief executive and the legislative branch is a common phenomenon even when both arms of government are in the control of the same party. Thus, a month ago (March 9, 1952) the President refused the House Judiciary Committee investigating corruption in government a list of the civil and criminal cases of the last six years in which the Department of Justice had decided to take no action although the data was certainly germane to the investigation. At the same time he indicated that he would make the material available to his own special investigator, Newbold Morris.[80] The Congress, however, unlike the courts, has weapons which it has not hesitated to use in such conflicts. By refusing to vote appropriations requested by the executive departments or by riders on appropriation acts restricting the use of funds the Congress has been able to maintain its own in such encounters. It has even attempted to prohibit the use of any funds for the salaries of specified officials.[81] Appropria-

---

[80] N. Y. *Herald Tribune,* March 9, 1952, p. 5; N. Y. *Times,* March 9, 1952, p. 82. Subsequent to the delivery of this lecture the President also refused to a congressional committee the diaries of the late Secretary of the Navy Forrestal, parts of which have already been published. N. Y. *Times,* May 1, 1952, p. 1.

[81] Congress made such an attempt in the Urgent Deficiency Appropria-

tion committees, moreover, frequently indicate to the heads of the executive departments that they will not appropriate money for certain functions unless those functions are performed in a particular manner; generally a word to the wise is sufficient. All this is in a way a recrudescence of the power exercised by the English House of Commons in the Middle Ages, of refusing a grant of funds to the Crown unless it yielded to Parliament in matters in dispute between them. While the power of the purse is its ordinary weapon, it is not to be forgotten that the Congress in the reconstruction era attempted to overthrow a chief executive by impeaching President Andrew Johnson.[82]

Tension in the federal government between the executive branch and the judicial, in which the Congress has more than once sided with the executive, runs back to the time of President Jefferson. Chief Justice Marshall's opinion in *Marbury v. Madison*,[83] upholding the power of the courts to set aside legislative acts in conflict with the Constitution, had infuriated Jefferson, who dominated both branches of the Congress. He was, however, unable to act at the moment because of the constitutional difficulties involved in the Louisiana Purchase[84] and his own impending re-election. The impeachment of Marshall's colleague, Justice Samuel

tion Act of 1943, 57 Stat. 450 (1943), but it was declared unconstitutional by the Supreme Court as a bill of attainder, *United States v. Lovett,* 328 U.S. 303 (1946).

[82] *The Great Impeachment Trial of Andrew Johnson* (Philadelphia, 1868); 2 Curtis, *Constitutional History of the United States* 696-703 (New York, 1896); 2 Hockett, *The Constitutional History of the United States* 347-355 (New York, 1939).

[83] 1 Cranch 137 (U.S. 1803).

[84] 3 Beveridge, *The Life of John Marshall 149* (Boston & New York, 1919). In a letter to Madison, Jefferson said: "The less we say about constitutional difficulties respecting Louisiana the better . . . . What is necessary for surmounting them must be done sub-silentio." *Ibid.*

Chase, was recognized by all, however, as a mere prelude to the impeachment of all the other justices of the Supreme Court.[85] Senator Giles, who prepared the rules for the trial, held that the Senate in impeachment proceedings did not act as a court: "Removal by impeachment was nothing more than a declaration by Congress to this effect: You hold dangerous opinions, and if you are suffered to carry them into effect you will work the destruction of the Nation." [86] He stated that in the administration's view impeachment "is nothing more than an enquiry, by the two Houses of Congress, whether the office of any public man might not be better filled by another." [87] The Senate's verdict of "not guilty" put an end to a theory of judicial tenure which would have meant the annihilation of an independent judiciary and the end of constitutional government. The verdict did not, however, end the struggle between President Jefferson and his cousin, Chief Justice Marshall. Thus, Jefferson left no stone unturned in his efforts to frustrate the *subpoena duces tecum* directed to him by Chief Justice Marshall in the trial of Aaron Burr.[88]

President Lincoln and the Supreme Court were at odds over the extent of the chief executive's power as commander-in-chief of the armed forces,[89] and President Theodore Roosevelt's campaign, first for the recall of judges and then for the recall of judicial decisions,[90] was matched only by President Franklin D. Roose-

[85] *Id.,* 160.

[86] *Id.,* 158.

[87] 3 Beveridge, *op. cit.,* 173.

[88] *Id.,* 433-456, 518-522.

[89] 2 Hockett, *op. cit.,* 288-307; Swisher, *Roger B. Taney* 540-556, 567-572 (New York, 1935); 3 Warren, *The Supreme Court in United States History* 90-96, 140-176 (Boston, 1922).

[90] Ransom, *Majority Rule and the Judiciary* (New York, 1912) with an introduction by Theodore Roosevelt; 3 Warren, *The Supreme Court in United States History, id.,* 465; Rogers, *American Bar Leaders* XI (Chi-

velt's court-packing plan.[91] Recently President Truman instructed the Secretary of Commerce to disregard the decisions of the courts directing the return of the Dollar Line to its owners.[92] In these encounters the judiciary has no weapons other than the shield of its own integrity and such support as may rally to it from an aroused public fearful of the peril to its liberties.

The most recent challenge came only ten days ago (April 8, 1952) in the President's seizure of the steel mills in a labor dispute in which he had declined to resort to the provisions of the Taft-Hartley Act.[93] This action of the President strikes not only at the right of a person not "to be deprived of life, liberty or property without due process of law," [94] but at the power of Congress to legislate and of the courts to adjudicate with respect to such rights. The claim has been boldly made that the President's power to act, in contradistinction to the powers of the Congress and of the courts, has no constitutional restrictions on it because no limitations are expressly set forth as to him, while they are as to the other two branches.[95] The idea is novel in American jurisprudence and while it is always unsafe to prophesy the outcome of any litigation, I cannot imagine that our courts

cago, 1932); Brown, Rome G., *Reports of Committee to Oppose Judicial Recall,* 38 A.B.A. Rep. 579-604 (1913), 39 A.B.A. Rep. 607-621 (1914), 40 A.B.A. Rep. 518-527 (1915), 41 A.B.A. Rep. 553-556 (1916), 42 A.B.A. Rep. 440-444 (1917), 43 A.B.A. Rep. 85-87 (1918).

[91] Corwin, *The President, Office and Powers* 351-353, 510-512 (3d ed., New York, 1948); Alsop & Catledge, *The 168 Days* (New York, 1938).

[92] See *Land v. Dollar,* 341 U.S. 737 (1951) at 740-748, where Justice Frankfurter in a memorandum gives a history of the proceedings.

[93] N. Y. *Times,* Apr. 9, 1952, p. 1; N. Y. *Herald Tribune,* Apr. 9, 1952, p. 1; N. Y. *Times,* Apr. 10, 1952, p. 28.

[94] U.S. Const. Amend. V.

[95] N. Y. *Times,* Apr. 16, 1952, p. 23. See also N. Y. *Times,* Apr. 26, 1952, p. 1, and N. Y. *Herald Tribune,* Apr. 26, 1952, p. 1.

will be disposed to accept the Roman concept of an emperor—a concept that has so plagued countries in which the civil law is administered notwithstanding their constitutional commitments to the doctrine of the separation of powers. It is hard to see how the case can fail to come in due course before the Supreme Court for a decision on its merits. The issues are so fundamental, so pressing, and so inescapable that it is inconceivable that the Court will attempt to dispose of them by resorting to the doctrine of judicial deference, of which I will speak presently. If I am correct in this view, we may expect one of the most momentous decisions on constitutional questions in the annals of the Court.[96] In adjudicating on the rights of the individual plaintiffs the Court must not only pass on the source and scope of the powers of the chief executive and his relation to the Congress with respect thereto, but also on the power of the judiciary in a proper case to review the acts of the President. Little did I imagine when I started to prepare these lectures that a case of such magnitude would arise

[96] Events that have transpired since the delivery of this lecture on April 18, 1952, necessitate special mention: On April 29th Judge Pine of the United States District Court for the District of Columbia held the seizure unconstitutional and on the following day issued a preliminary injunction restraining the Secretary of Commerce from continuing the seizure and possession of the mills, *Youngstown Sheet & Tube Co. v. Sawyer*, 103 F.S. 569. Within minutes of this decision the United Steel Workers Union declared a strike. On the same day the Court of Appeals for the District of Columbia stayed the injunction. See *Sawyer v. United States Steel Co.*, 197 F. 2d 582 (C.A. D.C., 1952). On May 2d the strike was called off and the following day the Supreme Court granted *certiorari*, 343 U.S. 937, 72 S. Ct. 775. Argument was had before the Supreme Court on May 12th and 13th and on June 2d it handed down its decision holding the seizure unconstitutional, thereby affirming the judgment of the District Court, 343 U.S. 597, 72 S. Ct. 863. Again the union promptly went on strike.

The multiplicity of opinions filed by the Supreme Court (eight in all:

so soon to test the vitality of the doctrine of the separation of powers.

In the light of the tremendous growth in the power and activities of the federal government, especially in the executive branch, has the judiciary measured up to its full responsibility as the arbiter under the Constitution of the scope of federal power as against state power, of executive power as against legislative power, and

majority opinion by Justice Black, two concurring opinions by Justice Frankfurter, concurring opinions by Justices Jackson, Burton, Clark and Douglas, and a dissenting opinion by Chief Justice Vinson in which Justices Reed and Minton joined) reveal a disappointing lack of agreement in the high court on certain of the basic issues involved. But this much is clear: the President may not unilaterally abrogate the protections extended to private property by the Fifth Amendment to the Constitution even in a self-declared emergency but is subject to judicial restraint. The door has not been finally closed, however, on the concept that, in certain emergencies, similar presidential action may be taken provided it is not forbidden in indisputable language by the Congress or the Constitution. Particularly disturbing is the fact that apparently only Justices Douglas, Frankfurter and Jackson finally agreed with Justice Black's statement with respect to the doctrine of the separation of power: "In the framework of our Constitution, the President's power to see that the laws are faithfully executed refutes the idea that he is to be a lawmaker. The Constitution limits his functions in the law-making process to the recommending of laws he thinks wise and the vetoing of laws he thinks bad. And the Constitution is neither silent nor unequivocal about who shall make laws which the President is to execute . . . . The Founders of this Nation entrusted the law-making power to the Congress alone in both good and bad times." 343 U.S. at 587-589, 72 S. Ct. at p. 867. Despite its limitations, however, the decision in this case is a significant victory in the fight to restore the proper balance between the three branches of the federal government, an important battle has been won, though not the war.

For an interesting account of the steel mills seizure from the comparative point of view, see Schwartz, *Inherent Executive Power and the Steel Seizure Case: A Landmark in American Constitutional Law,* 30 Can. B. Rev. 466 (1952).

of any and all governmental power against the rights of the individual citizen? Or has the judiciary in an era of expanding governmental activities, marked in many other countries by personal government rather than by rule of law, been unduly self-denying in exercising its constitutional responsibilities? And has it in its self-restraint not only deprived individuals of their constitutional rights but also endangered the balance of powers intended by the Constitution? There are several aspects of this self-imposed doctrine of judicial deference. We have already referred to the acquiescence of the federal courts in the action of Congress in denying essential judicial powers to courts. Is it possible to conceive of a court of equity without any injunctive power whatever any more than one may imagine a court of law without any power to entertain the defense in a criminal action that the law alleged to be violated is invalid? Yet the federal courts have conceded in certain cases, as we have seen, the power of the Congress to curtail their injunctive powers, to preclude access by an aggrieved individual to both the state and regular federal courts, and to adjudicate as to the validity of statutes and administrative regulations.

The doctrine of judicial deference has been applied increasingly to the work of the administrative agencies. First, the courts deferred to administrative findings of fact if there was "substantial evidence" to support them, reviewing only questions of law. Then, although the construction of statutes is peculiarly a function of the courts, they deferred to the administrative construction of statutes —a concession not made, of course, to trial courts which, not having legislative, investigatory and prosecuting functions, are obviously far more impartial and qualified than an administrative agency with such powers could humanly be to construe its own enabling acts or regulations. Finally, the courts deferred to the administrative agencies on mixed questions of law and fact.[97]

A curious offshoot of judicial deference to administrative judgment resulted from the reorganization by statute of the Board of Tax Appeals as the Tax Court. As a board, and hence as an administrative agency, it had the benefit of the rule of judicial deference which, as we have seen, has been so much expanded in recent years. As a court, it became, presumably, subject to the same judicial review on appeal as all other courts. Notwithstanding the undoubted judicial character of the Tax Court, the Supreme Court announced in 1943 in the *Dobson* case[98] a rule of continued deference to it.[99] The rule plagued all concerned with tax matters so much[100] that the Congress disposed of it legislatively,[101] but it lives on in other phases of administrative law.

[97] *Gray v. Powell,* 314 U.S. 402 (1941).

[98] *Dobson v. Commissioner,* 320 U.S. 489 (1943), *rehearing denied,* 321 U.S. 231 (1944).

[99] The Supreme Court, however, declined to extend the rule of finality applied to the Tax Court in the *Dobson* case to the District of Columbia Board of Tax Appeals; in such cases the court can review as to both facts and law. *District of Columbia v. Pace,* 320 U.S. 698, 64 S. Ct. 406 (1944).

[100] *Trust of Bingham v. Commissioner,* 325 U.S. 365, 65 S. Ct. 1232 (1945); *Cochran v. Commissioner,* 163 F. 2d 153 (C.C.A. 3d, 1947); *Survaunt v. Commissioner,* 162 F. 2d 753 (C.C.A. 8th, 1947); *Wichita Terminal El. Co. v. Commissioner,* 162 F. 2d 513 (C.C.A. 10th, 1947); *Eisenberg v. Commissioner,* 161 F. 2d 506 (C.C.A. 3d, 1947); *Hastings Mfg. Co. v. Federal Trade Commission,* 153 F. 2d 253 (C.C.A. 6th, 1946); *Adams v. Commissioner,* 155 F. 2d 246 (C.C.A. 3d, 1946); *Spirella Co., Inc. v. Commissioner,* 155 F. 2d 908 (C.C.A. 2d, 1946); *Heidenreich, Scope of Judicial Review of Decisions of the United States Tax Court,* 29 Minn. L. Rev. 186 (1945); Griswold, *The Need for a Court of Tax Appeals,* 57 Harv. L. Rev. 1153 (1944); Paul, *Dobson v. Commissioner: The Strange Ways of Law and Fact,* 57 Harv. L. Rev. 753 (1944); Note, 60 Harv. L. Rev. 448 (1947).

[101] 62 Stat. 991 (1948), 26 U.S.C. § 1141(a) (Supp. 1949), as amended, 63 Stat. 107 (1949), 26 U.S.C. § 1141(a) (Supp. 1950).

By such judicial deference the courts have narrowed the scope of judicial review of administrative action to issues of congressional power, of statutory authority, and the basic prerequisites of proof. It is difficult to find a logical justification for the distinction made by the courts between the full review accorded to the findings of fact and the conclusions of law of a chancellor experienced in the trial of equity cases and the limited review of the decision of an administrative expert who, in the language of Laski, is "saved from disaster only by the need of deference to the plain man's common sense." [102] The situation is, of course, far more dangerous if one is dealing with an *ex-officio* expert or, worse yet, a political transient craving preference rather than a genuine expert. Anyone who has had any experience in the trial of cases, either at the bar or on the bench, realizes that generally there is more difficulty in ascertaining the facts of a case than the law. Perspective as to the facts is more difficult to obtain at the trial level even for the capable and conscientious judge or administrator than it is on review. No wonder then that we find Chief Justice Hughes declaring:

> The power of administrative bodies to make findings of fact which may be treated as conclusive, if there is evidence both ways, is a power of enormous consequence. An unscrupulous administrator might be tempted to say, "Let me find the facts for the people of my country, and I care little who lays down the general principles." [103]

In the *St. Joseph Stock Yards* case the Chief Justice, who was no opponent of administrative agencies,[104] amplified this thought:

[102] Laski, *The Limitations of the Expert,* 162 *Harper's* Magazine 101, 109 (Dec., 1930).

[103] Address to the Federal Bar Association, N. Y. *Times,* Feb. 13, 1931, p. 18.

[104] *Ibid.,* see also Pusey, II *Charles Evans Hughes* 706 (New York, 1951).

Legislative agencies, with varying qualifications, work in a field peculiarly exposed to political demands. Some may be expert and impartial, others subservient.[105]

There is much force to the protest of United States Circuit Judge Waller. In a strong attack upon the very basis of the substantial evidence rule, he asserted that the courts which cannot review both law and facts are denied "the judicial power" that has been conferred upon them under the Constitution:

Give a partisan examiner or board the right to fix the facts and the right to declare the law may well be but as "sounding brass or a tinkling cymbal." . . . If the judicial power is vested in the courts in all cases and controversies mentioned in Section 2 of Article III; if a review by a Federal court of the decision of a board is a case or a controversy; if the judicial power is the power to administer justice; and if in the administration of justice it is necessary first to know the truth, how can Congress constitutionally withhold from the courts on review the right to be satisfied as to facts? [106]

To make a full review on both law and facts available would not mean that our federal appellate courts must apply it on every appeal, but is it not in the interest of justice that they be given the power to do so when it is made to appear by brief or argument that justice so requires? In any event, is there any reason why the state courts should follow the federal example? They necessarily hear appeals from many local boards of inexperienced laymen who cannot be expected to have even the limited competence

---

[105] *St. Joseph Stock Yards Co. v. U. S.*, 298 U.S. 38, 52 (1936).

[106] Specially concurring in *National Labor Relations Board v. Robbins Tire and Rubber Co.*, 161 F. 2d 798, 804 (C.C.A. 5th, 1947).

of *ex-officio* experts. Furthermore, most of the state courts, being constitutional courts with fixed jurisdiction, cannot be legislatively limited as to the kind of review that they will afford litigants.

The self-imposed judicial limitation on a full review of law and fact affects more than the individual cases the courts may have under consideration. The full force of the substantial evidence rule on particular cases and on administrative activities generally cannot be gathered from a consideration of Supreme Court decisions alone. To understand the effect of the rule, one must look into the workings of the system of review by *certiorari* in the Supreme Court. If an administrative decision is clearly without basis in the record and the lower courts hold it invalid, the government may not attempt to carry the case up to the Supreme Court or the latter may refuse to review it, even if so requested, on an application for a writ of *certiorari*. The result of this process is that cases where the agencies might be reversed seldom reach the Supreme Court, and accordingly reversals of administrative agencies there are rare. Superficially it appears from the Supreme Court reports that the agencies are almost always right, for nearly all reversals of agencies in the lower courts are in turn reversed by the Supreme Court. This result has had the effect, in turn, of dissuading original courts of review from upsetting administrative orders in any but the most extreme cases. Nor does this one-sided process of selectivity in the *certiorari* process end here; because of the disinclination of the Supreme Court to review cases of private wrong as distinguished from cases in which public agencies seek review, the failure of lower courts to exercise fully their powers of judicial review is rarely subjected to correction by the Supreme Court. The substantial evidence rule and the *certiorari* process are the millstones which threaten to crush the life out of judicial review as a reality while preserving its form.

Equally devastating to the individual litigant and the general public are many of the self-imposed limitations on judicial review of issues of constitutionality. Here, too, the doctrine of judicial deference has evolved gradually. Its classic formulation is to be found in the *Ashwander* case:

1. The Court will not pass on the constitutionality of legislation in a friendly, non-adversary, proceeding.
2. The Court will not "anticipate a question of constitutional law in advance of the necessity of deciding it."
3. The Court will not "formulate a rule of constitutional law broader than is required by the precise facts to which it is to be applied."
4. The Court will not pass upon a constitutional question . . . if there is also present some other ground upon which the case may be disposed of.
5. The Court will not pass upon the validity of a statute upon complaint of one who fails to show that he is injured by its operation.
6. The Court will not pass upon the constitutionality of a statute at the instance of one who has availed himself of its benefits.
7. "When the validity of an act . . . is drawn in question, and even if a serious doubt of constitutionality is raised, it is a cardinal principle that this Court will first ascertain whether a construction . . . is fairly possible by which the question may be avoided." [107]

One does not have to quarrel with all of these canons to wonder if Chief Justice Marshall's great opinion in *Marbury v. Madison*[108] would not have died stillborn and with it the judicial power to declare an act unconstitutional, if the great Chief Justice had been

[107] Concurring opinion of Justice Brandeis in *Ashwander v. Tennessee Valley Authority,* 297 U.S. 288, 346-348 (1936).
[108] 1 Cranch 137 (U.S. 1803), *supra.*

bound by these principles of self-abnegation. Rather must we not give heed to Marshall's pointed reference to the constitutional requirement that every judge be bound by oath or affirmation "to support this Constitution" [109]—not part of it, but all of it:

> Why otherwise does it direct the judges to take an oath to support it? This oath certainly applies in an especial manner, to their conduct in their official character. How immoral to impose it on them, if they were to be used as the instruments, and the knowing instruments, for violating what they swear to support! [110]

Can there be any doubt that on numerous important issues vital and pressing constitutional questions have gone unanswered because of undue judicial deference? In the *Ashwander* case, for example, stockholders were denied an adjudication of the validity of a contract between their corporation and the Tennessee Valley Authority. But perhaps the most dangerous instance of undue judicial deference, until very recent times, was the decision of the Supreme Court in *Massachusetts v. Mellon*,[111] which challenged the constitutionality of the Maternity Act, providing for appropriations of money to be allotted among the several states for the purpose of reducing maternal and infant mortality. The allotment to each state, in accordance with the accepted formula of grants-in-aid, was made conditional on acceptance by the states of the terms of the statute. The states, again in the normal pattern of grants-in-aid, were to contribute financially. Massachusetts claimed that the statute was unconstitutional as a usurpation of power reserved to the states under the Tenth Amendment. It was argued that even though the state had not accepted the Act, its constitu-

---

[109] U.S. Const. Art. VI, § 3.
[110] *Marbury v. Madison, op. cit.,* 178.
[111] 262 U.S. 447 (1923).

tional rights were infringed by the imposition of an option either to yield part of its reserved rights to the federal government or to lose its share of the appropriation. The cases (there was also a suit by an individual taxpayer tied with the state suit) were "disposed of for want of jurisdiction without considering the merits of the constitutional questions."[112] With respect to Massachusetts the Court said:

> In the last analysis, the complaint of the plaintiff State is brought to the naked contention that Congress has usurped the reserved powers of the several States by the mere enactment of the statute . . . ; and it is plain that that question, as it is thus presented, is political and not judicial in character, and therefore is not a matter which admits of the exercise of the judicial power.[113]
>
> No rights of the State falling within the scope of the judicial power have been brought within the actual or threatened operation of the statute and this Court is . . . without authority to pass abstract opinions upon the constitutionality of acts of Congress.[114]

The plaintiff taxpayer alleged that the effect of the statute would be to take her property, under the guise of taxation, without due process of law. Here, too, the Court declined to pass on the merits of the petition and asserted that an action does not lie by a taxpayer to test the constitutionality of an appropriation measure. Mere suffering "in some indefinite way in common with people generally" [115] is not sufficient interest, it was said by the Court, to invoke its jurisdiction. The substance of the plaintiff's complaint was stated by the court to be:

[112] *Massachusetts v. Mellon* and *Frothingham v. Mellon*, 262 U.S. 447, 480 (1923).

[113] *Id.*, 483.

[114] *Id.*, 485.

[115] *Massachusetts v. Mellon, op. cit.*, 488.

Merely that officials of the executive departments of the government are executing and will execute an act of Congress asserted to be unconstitutional; and this we are asked to prevent. To do so would be not to decide a judicial controversy, but to assume a position of authority over the governmental acts of another and co-equal department, an authority which plainly we do not possess.[116]

The net result is that notwithstanding the fact that the constitutional issue was raised by the only parties who could possibly object to the act, the United States Supreme Court avoided deciding it and thereby left unanswered one of the most important constitutional questions ever presented to it. By an act of self-imposed judicial deference the Court has rendered immune from attack the flood of legislative appropriations that have created an imbalance between the states and federal government never dreamed of by the Founding Fathers or the judges who spoke of "an indestructible Union, composed of indestructible States." [117]

Professor Oliver P. Field has summarized with restraint yet with clarity the situation in which the Court finds itself in applying its canon of "interest" for testing unconstitutionality:

The Court is still struggling with the problem of "interest" on the part of those who seek to challenge the validity of statutes. Little can be done to extricate the law from the bog into which it has fallen on this point so long as the idea prevails that constitutionality should be sparingly dealt with by the courts. It should be just the opposite, but with statutes or rules of limitation as to the time in which it could be done.[118]

[116] *Id.*, 488-489.
[117] *Texas v. White,* 7 Wall. 700, 725 (U.S. 1868).
[118] *Separation and Delegation of Powers,* 41 Am. Pol. Sci. Rev. 1161, 1168-1169 (1947), citing: "On moot case, see *St. Pierre v. United States,* 319 U.S. 41 (1943). On party without interest, see *Tileston v. Ullman,* 318 U.S. 44 (1943); *Ex parte Albert Levitt,* 302 U.S. 633 (1937). On

The doctrine of judicial deference has also served to prevent citizens from obtaining their full voting right. In *Colegrove v. Green* [119] the Supreme Court held itself without jurisdiction to decide a controversy involving the apportionment scheme of Illinois with respect to seats in Congress. The effect of the Illinois apportionment act was to give the citizens in some districts a vote disproportionate to that given citizens in other districts. The Court held that to invalidate a state redistricting statute would be to infringe on the exclusive power of Congress and the states to control the election of congressmen, saying:

> The Constitution has left the performance of many duties in our governmental scheme to depend on the fidelity of the executive and legislative action and, ultimately, on the vigilance of the people in exercising their political rights. [120]

In *South v. Peters* [121] the Supreme Court reaffirmed the doctrine of the *Colegrove* case and refused to consider a petition alleging that the county unit system in Georgia was unconstitutionally discriminatory by decreasing the effectiveness of votes from the populous areas. This case also raised the issue of racial discrimination in that the operation of the system permitted a virtual disenfranchisement of Negro voters. In these two cases, out of judicial deference to the action of the two state legislatures, the equal protection clause faded out of the Constitution and with it fundamental rights of citizens of Georgia and Illinois.

Must not situations such as those involved in the *Ashwander* and the *Mellon,* the *Colegrove* and the *South* cases be reconsidered

---

error in passing on constitutional question when case could be disposed of without considering it, see *Alma Motor Company v. Timken-Detroit Axle Company and United States,* 91 L. Ed. 150 (1946)."

[119] 328 U.S. 549 (1946).

[120] *Id.,* 556.

[121] 339 U.S. 276 (1950).

in the light of the enlarged powers of the Congress and of the President and the administrative agencies, all made possible by the new construction placed by the courts on the "general welfare" clause in the tax section of the legislative article of the Constitution?[122] And should not the Court, having made the welfare state possible, permit litigation of the issue of what is and what is not for the general welfare?[123] Has the time not come for a reconsideration of the propriety of the entire doctrine of judicial deference, if the balance contemplated by the Constitution is to be recovered? Should the weakest branch of government on its own initiative weaken itself still further at the expense of the clear rights of citizens under the Constitution?

[122] U.S. Const. Art. I, § 8. "The Congress shall have Power to lay and collect Taxes, Duties, Imposts and Excises, to pay the Debts and provide for the common Defence and general Welfare of the United States; but all Duties, Imposts and Excises shall be uniform throughout the United States." *Mulford v. Smith,* 307 U.S. 38, 59 S. Ct. 648 (1949); *Alabama Power Co. v. Ickes,* 302 U.S. 464, 58 S. Ct. 300 (1938); *Helvering v. Davis,* 301 U.S. 619, 57 S. Ct. 904 (1937); *Stewart Machine Co. v. Davis,* 301 U.S. 548, 57 S. Ct. 883 (1937); *United States v. Butler,* 297 U.S. 1, 56 S. Ct. 312 (1936).

[123] See *Sunshine Coal Co. v. Adkins,* 310 U.S. 381, 60 S. Ct. 907 (1940); *Tennessee Power Co. v. T. V. A.,* 306 U.S. 118, 59 S. Ct. 366 (1939); *Alabama Power Co. v. Ickes, id.; Helvering v. Davis, id.; Cincinnati Soap Co. v. U. S.,* 301 U.S. 308, 57 S. Ct. 764 (1937); *Sonzinsky v. U. S.,* 300 U.S. 506, 57 S. Ct. 554 (1937); Dodd *Cases and Materials on Constitutional Law* 505 (4th ed., St. Paul, 1949), where he says: "As the validity of a federal spending act can be attacked only by a state or by an individual, if both are disqualified, the legislation is substantially not subject to review. The position of the court leaves to congressional discretion the question of how money derived from taxes shall be expended;" Corwin, *Constitutional Revolution, Ltd.* 108 (Claremont, 1941), where he says: "The establishment of the New Deal upon an indefeasible constitutional basis has unquestionably crowded judicial review of acts of Congress into narrow quarters, and for a reason which is easily comprehended once it is pointed

The responsibility for the growth of federal powers at the expense of the states and for the increase in the powers of the executive branch of the federal government rests, in the first instance, on the Congress and, in the second place, on the federal judiciary. The Congress has delegated vast legislative powers to the executive branch and it has assumed broad powers to promote what it considers to be in the general welfare, all without review by the courts. The assumption by each branch of the government of its full responsibility—but no more—will be no easy task in view of the drift of events, but it is a task nevertheless that must be accomplished if we are to maintain constitutional government.

The doctrine of judicial deference is not the only force working to the disadvantage of the position of the courts. In a representative, democratic government such as ours the power of the judiciary depends largely on its reputation for independence, integrity and wisdom. All too often our judges, even in our courts of last resort, have weakened their position with the public by indulging in politics in clear violation of the Canons of Judicial Ethics[124] as

out. This is, that in *choosing from among the formulas, rules, or devices of constitutional law which I set forth in my opening lecture those formulas, rules, devices which favored the New Deal legislation, the Court then and there eliminated, and probably for an indefinite future, the competing and antagonistic formulas, rules, devices.* Not again for a long time will the Court hold void an act of Congress against which nothing can be said by way of constitutional objection except that it invades the accustomed field of state power and tends to upset the Federal Equilibrium. Not again for a long time will it set aside an act of Congress— any act that Congress is likely to pass—on the ground solely that it deprives persons of liberty 'unreasonably,' and so without 'due process of law.' In a word, those doctrines of constitutional law which have been hitherto the chief sources of its broadly supervisory powers over congressional legislation have simply dried up, at least for the time being. If they still retain the spark of life, it is at least dormant."

[124] "While entitled to entertain his personal views of political questions,

well as of the doctrine of the separation of powers. True, commendable progress has been made since 1777 when the Chief Justice of South Carolina began his charge to the Grand Jury with a long statement of the justice of the Revolution, its military successes and the duties of patriotism, whereupon the court ordered "that the political part of the Chief Justice's charge be forthwith printed,"[125] I have been informed by reliable authority, however, that within the past few weeks a justice of the Supreme Court of a nearby state circularized the bar of Nebraska in favor of the candidacy of one of his friends for the presidency of the United States. And it was only four years ago that a chief justice of one of our great commonwealths sat in the national convention of his party as a delegate at large and when a member of the bar challenged the propriety of his action, the chief justice refused to comment on the matter beyond calling his critic names. These, perhaps, are exceptional cases, yet it does the courts no good for this justice or that judge to be mentioned in the public press, as frequently happens, for political activity of one sort or another. The popular election of judges in partisan contests is the greatest obstacle to public respect for the judiciary because it is the most common vice in the judicial system. But whatever the shortcom-

and while not required to surrender his rights or opinions as a citizen, it is inevitable that suspicion of being warped by political bias will attach to a judge who becomes the active promoter of the interests of one political party as against another. He should avoid making political speeches, making or soliciting payment of assessments or contributions to party funds, the public endorsement of candidates for political office and participation in party conventions.

"He should neither accept nor retain a place on any party committee nor act as party leader, nor engage generally in partisan activities." Judicial Canon 28 of the Canons of Judicial Ethics of the American Bar Association (1947).

[125] Baldwin, *The American Judiciary, op. cit.,* 44.

ings of the bench in failing to live up to the Canons of Judicial Ethics may be, the bar must share in the blame, for the bar has, or at least it should have, the primary responsibility for the selection of judges from its midst.

From the high professional ideals which governed the bench and the bar in the immediate post-Revolutionary period we sank rapidly until in the second quarter of the nineteenth century we had reached the level of "to the victors belong the spoils," with judges in most states elected for short terms in bitter partisan campaigns. The road back to respectability has been long and hard. It was not until 1906 that the conscience of the profession was first aroused nationally by the great speech of Roscoe Pound at the American Bar Association meeting in St. Paul on *The Causes of Popular Dissatisfaction with the Administration of Justice.*[126] As Dean Wigmore said, it "kindled the white flame of progress . . . the soul of the profession had been touched."[127] Great strides forward have been made in the intervening half century since Dean Pound's address at St. Paul, but much remains to be done if we would adapt the law and government to the needs of the times. The situations that confront us in our life, nationally and throughout the world, are indeed momentous and some of them are without precedent. The problems of government are complicated and difficult of solution. But must it not be apparent to everyone, as we gaze into the future, that we cannot hope to maintain the way of life which we call American without exercising every effort to preserve to each branch of government its proper sphere and to the states and the Union a due recognition of their proper functions?

[126] 29 A.B.A. Rep. 395 (1906).
[127] Roscoe Pound's St. Paul Address of 1906, 20 J. Am. Jud. Soc'y 176-178 (1937).

The responsibility for the law *today* rests primarily on the bar and only to a slightly less extent on the bench. The responsibility for *tomorrow* rests heavily on the colleges and the law schools. If we are frank, who can deny that our colleges have been favoring natural science and vocational training at the expense of teaching the science of government and the art of politics, or that the law schools have been specializing on private law for the benefit of our commercial civilization at the expense of serving the states and the nation through the adequate teaching of public law? If Laski is right—and who can deny the soundness of his thesis— the public welfare depends as much on enlightening the plain man's common sense as it does on educating the expert at the bar or on the bench, in the executive office or the legislative hall.

We must move forward. We cannot be slaves to the past. But this does not mean that we may not learn much from the mistakes of others, or that we should not avoid making the same mistakes twice ourselves in adapting our law and government to the changing needs of the times. The development of the doctrine of the separation of powers in England and in this country was not worked out in the study, but in contests with the king on the field of battle, in the legislative chambers, and in the courts of law. There would seem to be no reason for our throwing overboard whatever is sound in this hard-earned experience. Nor in our efforts at home should we shut our eyes to the fate of the individual citizen in those countries that have abandoned or give merely lip service to the doctrine of the separation of powers. On respect for the doctrine of the separation of powers, not as a technical rule of law but as a guide to the sound functioning of government, rests not only the stability of this nation but of every other nation and the freedom not only of our own citizens but of the citizens of every other country. The doctrine must be universal in its application if stability and liberty are to be sought and obtained.